LA_{UGH}T_ER

from the **Hip**

The Lighter Side of Jazz

LAUGHTER

from the Hip

The Lighter Side of Jazz

by Leonard Feather and Jack Tracy

drawings by A. BIRNBAUM

with a new introduction by **Leonard Feather**

A DACAPO PAPERBACK

Library of Congress Cataloging in Publication Data

Feather, Leonard G
   Laughter from the hip.

   (A Da Capo paperback)
   1. Music — Anecdotes, facetiae, satire, etc.
2 Jazz music. I. Tracy, Jack, joint author.
II. Title.
[ML65.F4   1979]   785.4'2'0207   78-20845
ISBN 0-306-80092-6

ISBN 0-306-80092-6

First Paperback Edition 1979

This Da Capo Press paperback edition of *Laughter From the Hip* is an unabridged republication of the first edition published by Horizon Press in New York in 1963. It is reprinted by arrangement with Horizon Press.

Published by Da Capo Press, Inc.
A Subsidiary of Plenum Publishing Corporation
227 West 17th Street, New York, N.Y. 10011

INTRODUCTION TO THE 1979 EDITION

The quality of humor is not strained; in jazz, its essence lingers on forever.

When *Laughter From The Hip* was first published sixteen years ago, the concept of a book about jazz that failed to take itself very seriously seemed somehow reprehensible to many observers (among them some of the most influential critics, who ignored it rather than lend it the dignity of a review). As a consequence, very few of those who might have savored these pages of comedy relief were aware that *Laughter from the Hip* existed.

I am delighted, and Jack Tracy shares my pleasure, that Da Capo Press has seen fit to draw belated attention to a work that dares to take itself lightly. It seems to me that these anecdotes and satires are more than mere comedy for its own sake; they tell us something about the times we live in and the men and women who populate the world of jazz.

With very few exceptions, such as the bebopper items, the contents have withstood the test of time. Many of the great artists about or by whom the stories were told are no longer with us: one of the most recent losses was the man we selected to lead off our first chapter, Joe Venuti. He seemed to symbolize all that was self-mocking and irreverent about many jazz musicians. The appreciation of his consummate artistry was in no way reduced by the legendary practical jokes associated with him.

Duke and Dinah and Nat Cole and too many others are gone, yet whatever was amusing about the stories that involve them retains its meaning today. I am sure that if Hollywood were to make *The Duke Ellington Story* even now, it might very well work out just the way I imagined it in my scenario.

Jazz at times has tended to be pompous, and jazz criticism in particular often takes itself so seriously that the reader may be disconcerted, even turned off by its pretentiousness. In

Laughter from the Hip there was no attempt to prove anything except that there has always been room, in the jazz world we have inhabited for most of our lives, for a touch of wit and drollery to help preserve our sanity. If that point was made in 1963, I'm sure it is valid today.

LEONARD FEATHER
Sherman Oaks, California
1979

ACKNOWLEDGMENTS

Special thanks are due to Whitey Mitchell, André Previn, David Raksin, Charlie Barnet, Kay Starr, Patricia Willard, Shorty Sherock, Joe Morgen, Mike Gould, and the many others who gladly gave up hours of their time to lend weight to this weightless project.

The three pieces by Professor McSiegel, and *The Duke Ellington Story*, are reproduced by permission of *Down Beat* Magazine.

Thanks to Dean Jennings for permission to use material from his not-yet-published biography of George Shearing.

- To Jane Feather who dreamed up the whole idea and Eleanor Tracy who agreed

CONTENTS

1

Cast of characters

Joe Venuti

Count Basie

Dave Brubeck

Dizzy Gillespie

Benny Goodman

Vido Musso

Wingy Manone

Eddie Condon

George Shearing

Duke Ellington

Now, infidel, I have thee on the hip!

William Shakespeare, *The Merchant of Venice*

JOE VENUTI

Joe Venuti has become a legend in his own time as a practical joker, heckler, clown, and, by the way, superlative jazz violinist.

His sense of humor has been a source of amazement to musicians for more than thirty years. Once he played a joke at his own expense that served no purpose, but helped relieve the unemployment situation.

One day he called 37 bass fiddle players and told them all to meet him Saturday at 8 p.m. at the northeast corner of 52nd Street and Broadway. The men showed up, lugging their basses, and made the sidewalk impassable.

Venuti merely drove around the block several times, roaring with laughter at the weird scene he had created.

Incredibly, he paid a night's fee to every one of the bassists.

Then there was the time in 1936 when both Joe's band and Paul Whiteman's orchestra played at the Texas Centennial in Dallas. Each night Whiteman would start the program with the entire stadium darkened except for a small spotlight on him while he conducted *The Star-Spangled Banner* with a lighted baton.

One day Venuti bribed the electrician to throw the spot on him, instead. What the audience saw was Venuti, dressed only in long underwear, conducting the orchestra with a fishing pole, at the end of which was an electric light bulb.

So many and widely-varied (and sometimes incredible) are the stories about Venuti, we thought we'd let the witnesses tell them in their own words. Such as . . .

Kay Starr: My greatest musical education was during my four years with the Venuti band.

In one town we visited, the manager of the place we were supposed to play came up to Joe and said, "There's a War Bond drive on, and they want you to play a broadcast at the local radio station."

Well, we had just finished setting up the bandstand, and it would all have to be taken down again and hauled to the station so Joe was just a little hacked about it. But we took it down and showed up at the station.

During the War Bond days they were forever putting people in charge of shows of this kind who really didn't know what it was all about. The least musically knowledgeable people were put in charge of things that needed the most imagination. We got one of those colonels or majors or something who was very smitten with his own importance. And there's nothing that annoys Joe more than somebody that's in an important position and doesn't deserve to be there.

This fellow is telling Joe things like, "You're not playing enough fast songs and too many slow songs." All of a sudden he was a music director.

All we wanted to do was do the show and get out of there and have a few minutes' rest before we did our regular show, because we'd been driving all night and we were all dead tired. So Joe says, "Okay, feller, just tell me what you want."

The major goes into the control room. Now he wants to check the sound level on everything. Then he starts this routine with, "No, the saxophones are too close," and "Joe, back a little further," until finally Joe couldn't take it any more. And he says, "We're going to have to take a rest."

So we all went out in the hall with him, and he says: "I'm going to fix this s.o.b., this two-bit Marconi. Now here's what we'll do. We'll go back in there and do like we're going to do the whole show, and I want everybody to go through the motions of everything they're supposed to do, but I don't want a single sound to come out of anybody."

So we all troop back in, and Joe says, "Okay, let's get this show on the road." And we start out. Joe kicks it off, and I wish you could have seen the expression on the faces in the control booth. The major has the earphones on, and he's taking the earphones off and banging them and saying to the other fellows in the booth, "Can you hear anything?" And they've got these dials all set and they're flipping them around and going out of their minds trying to figure out why the sound's gone dead.

Meanwhile, a saxophone player is going through all these crazy contortions, looking like he was really playing a wild hot chorus, but of course nothing was coming out. And then I got up and "sang" the chorus I was supposed to do, and I'd smile at them in the booth as if to say, "How's it coming through?" And the fellows are signaling: "Get closer! Get closer!"

Finally this major had banged his earphones so hard they fell apart . . . they were completely wrecked. And the other guy had changed so many levers and everything, and two-and-a-half hours after we'd arrived there for rehearsal they couldn't put that show on the air. They had just about torn up the whole control room.

Then Joe says, "Well, we can't stay any longer," and we left them, with everyone still working on the dials.

It was no more than the major deserved, but I've often felt sorry for those technicians and wondered whether they ever found out what was really the matter.

:

Once we had to play an outdoor job in a bandshell near Toledo. It was one of those late spring days and people were dressed kind of summery, and we figured these people knew more about the local weather than we did. So I put on my evening gown and the fellows wore their summer jackets. And of course it turned freezing cold.

A cold horn, of course, means just one thing: you blow completely out of tune. Every time a fellow went up to play a chorus he couldn't just say, "Stop, I have to tune up first." It was murderous. So Joe says, "We can't have this."

At that time we used a lot of stock arrangements, because there wasn't any money to buy special arrangements. Joe took a whole bunch of the stocks that he didn't like, put them in a wheelbarrow, and broke up a whole bunch of wooden crates—everyone was scared to death he'd take the music stands and the horns

4

next—and set fire to the whole thing, right there on the bandstand.

Every guy, before he took his chorus on the air, would go to the fire, warm his hands, warm his horn, go in the corner, tune up, and take his solo. Afterwards the fire came in handy for dinner, too. We roasted hot dogs on it.

:

Joe was with Paul Whiteman during the time Mildred Bailey was singing with the band. Mildred was very attached to her two dachshunds, Hans and Fritz. When they got to a hotel she'd always rent an adjoining room and bath. Nobody ever knew what it was for, until it got to be very hot in the summer, and she let people in on it: it was so the dogs could have their own bathroom. She'd run two or three inches of water in the tub, and leave them in there. Their legs were so short that they'd have cool bellies, if nothing else.

Mildred's birthday was coming up, and the guys didn't know what to get her, because she had everything. They figured the only thing left was to do something crazy. The two presents they decided on almost led to the police being called in. They couldn't get them in the elevator, so they had to drag them up four flights of stairs, and finally they got them there and left them outside her room with a note saying: "Happy birthday to you and your children."

They'd bought a pair of matching trees—each about forty feet tall.

:

Joe tells another story about the time he was with Paul Whiteman. That was a particularly crazy era, around 1928, and everybody had all the money they could use and more. One year Whiteman gave each of the guys in the band a car, and a matching one for their wives.

The fellows used to place bets on everything. So they checked into this hotel, and they're on the 17th floor, and somebody says, "I've got an idea . . . Let's take this piano and heave it out the window, and we'll make book on what note it'll hit." They all

5

got together, pushed the piano out the window and it landed in the courtyard. I don't know what note it hit, but I don't suppose they had too much trouble finding out, as they were all prepared. They had a tuning fork.

:

As you know, Don D'Arcy got to be quite well-known during the 1940s as a band singer. The story of how his career began is almost unbelievable, but I saw it happen.

During a tour with Venuti, we were in a caravan of cars. One day we stopped to check a contract and Joe looked at it and said, "My God! I'm supposed to have a boy singer with the band tonight!"

Everybody starts asking one another: "Can you sing? Can you sing?" But they decided that a horn-player just doubling as a vocalist probably wouldn't satisfy the promoter; the contract called for a male and female vocalist in addition to the whole band.

We stopped to eat at one of those little roadside places, and there was a kid sitting at the end of the counter. He was kind of seedy looking, and he was sitting there with five or six empty plates around him. It looked as though he was keeping track of how many pieces of pie he'd eaten.

Joe was intrigued. He sat next to the kid and saw him finish nine or ten pieces of pie. He started a conversation with him and said, "If you can eat five more pieces of pie, I'll pay for all of them." So the kid ordered five more pieces and ate them all.

Joe got a good laugh out of it and didn't mind paying. Then he says to this kid, "What do you do? You got a job?" The kid says, "No, I'm not working." "Can you drive a truck?" Joe asks him. He says: "I can do anything." Joe says, "Get a load of this kid! He can do anything! Can you sing?"

"Sure," says the kid. "What do you want me to sing?"

"You're all set," says Joe. "You can drive the truck, and you can sing on this next job." Joe let him have the truck with all our music and a thousand dollars' worth of instruments in it—he didn't know him from Adam; the kid could have driven off with the truck—but we all got to this next town. Joe still hadn't heard the kid sing.

Joe went out and rented a tuxedo for him, and bought him a dickey, and tied a rubber band from the bottom of the dickey to the top of his pants, so that when he'd swell his chest out the rubber band would expand. The kid just had cuffs, a dickey, and this tuxedo.

"All right," said Joe. "Now what do you want to sing?"

"I told you—I'll sing whatever you want me to sing."

"What you got, a high or a low voice?"

"I got a *good* voice."

It was a small-town theater. They figured out a key on *Ol' Man River*. Finally, when he saw the spotlight and the stage, the kid gets a little meeker. "What'll I do if I forget the words?" "Just sing anything," said Joe, "only remember one thing: whatever you do, don't panic—sing! Just walk to the middle of the stage— if you want to rehearse, I'll practice with you."

"I don't need any practice," he said. "I'll get it."

Well, Don did the show—and he sang fine. But when he first came out of the wings and the spotlight hit him he went into such a state of shock that he kept walking and walking to the front of the stage, and walked clear off until he fell into the orchestra pit, ten or twelve feet below. Crash! Bam! Bang! You never heard such a commotion. The band was up on the stage, and down in the pit was nothing but chairs, music stands and boxes and stuff—and Don.

Our men were busy playing and didn't even see all this. They finished playing the introduction, when all of a sudden, from the bottom of the pit, they heard:

"Ol' man river . . . that ol' man river . . ."

Joe covered up fast when he saw what had happened, and he took the band into another number real fast. After the show the manager of the theater came up and threw his arms around Joe and said, "Wonderful! That's the greatest act I've ever seen!"

Don limped for a while, but nothing was broken. No audience has ever seen an entrance like that before or since.

Zeke Zarchy: One day on "The Edgar Bergen Show" we got to telling Venuti stories. I asked the guys if they'd ever heard about the sax player who tried out for him. After letting him sit around most of the night, Joe finally motioned to the guy and said, "Take a chorus, kid."

The guy got up, took one, took another, and another . . . Joe kept him playing 20 minutes until the kid's eyes were bugging out and he started repeating the same licks over and over. Finally he gave up. And Joe said, "Now go out and change my tire."

The guys laughed skeptically when I told this story. But one of them, Bob Romeo, said, "I believe you. I was the saxophonist."

Ed Kelly: One night Joe had a saxophone player who kept tapping his foot slightly off the beat. Joe couldn't stand it. He went out and got a hammer and nail and nailed the guy's shoe to the stand.

Tommy Gumina: Venuti once was on a television show that was sponsored by a hair cream. The show began to bug him after a while, so once, in the middle of a live commercial, he bent over, showed his big bald spot to the camera, and said, "This is what ———— Cream Oil did for me."

The sponsor dropped the show.

Irving Edelman: Once Joe got into a fight with a guy who'd been giving him a bad time and the guy brought him up on charges of assault and battery. This was in a small town, and the magistrate looked down at Joe and said, "I've got your records, Mr. Venuti." Joe got alarmed and thought maybe they'd trumped-up a police record on him. But then it turned out that the judge was an ex-fiddle player and a big fan of Venuti's, and he had all his phonograph records. The judge told the other guy off and threw the case out of court.

•

Most typical of him, though, was the incident at the Lakeside golf club in Hollywood one day, when after hitting a ball into the water several times, Joe lost his always-limited patience.

He threw the club he'd been using into the lake, then threw the rest of the bag in after it, then picked up the caddie and threw him in, and finally jumped in himself.

COUNT BASIE

The swing era involved a clear trend toward bigger bands and a greater degree of organization. But the Basie band, created during the middle 1930s, has outlasted all others. The group was famous for the informality from which it drew much of its strength.

"When I first joined the Basie band," recalls the trumpeter Harry "Sweets" Edison, "I couldn't read music." Since I was going to make music my career, I wanted to read music and learn more about it. But they kept playing and playing until I didn't know where I was. Finally I said, "Hey, Basie, where are we?" And he answered, "What's the matter? 'You're *playing*, aren't you?' So I said, 'Yeah, but I want to know *what* I'm playing. When the band ends, I don't know what note to hit.' Then Basie told me, 'If you hit a note tonight and it sounds right, just play that same note tomorrow!' "

During this period (1937) the arrangements were not even known by that name; according to early sidemen, the few scores available were called "frame-ups." The Basie library was so small, says Edison, that "we used to carry the entire thing, everybody's parts, in one little portfolio. We took turns; one night I'd carry it in my trumpet case, the next night Jo Jones would put it in with his drums, another night Ed Lewis or Herschel Evans would carry it. Boy, we didn't need a valet in those days. But when it came to Lester Young's turn to carry the book, he'd balk. When we asked him where the music was, he'd say, 'Well, if you don't know your parts, I know mine!' "

Though he has a remarkable memory for events in the distant past, Basie at times can be as absentminded as Benny Goodman. "One thing you can be sure about on a road tour with this band," Basie's veteran road manager Henry Snodgrass once commented,

9

"Basie won't know where he's going, who he's playing for, or how to get there." On one occasion in 1945 Sarah Vaughan, still almost unknown and eager for a job as vocalist with the Count, applied for an audition while the orchestra was playing at the Roxy Theater. Basie casually assigned her to a dressing room backstage, where she played piano accompanying half a dozen other singers who also wanted to audition; then just as casually he dismissed her, voice unheard.

A one-night stand for the Basie band, as for others, may be an occasion for a happy reunion with old friends, or it may be an evening-long ordeal in an overgrown watershed where the fungus crawls on the dressing room walls and the acoustics are designed for lip-readers. Basie shows a sense of humor even in these circumstances. On more than one occasion he has been known to open the evening's first set with an old Duke Ellington composition that bears an apt title of which most of the audience is unaware: *What Am I Here For?*

The loss of clothes, baggage and horns as a consequence of the rush between one-nighters is practically standard operating procedure. Perhaps the most remarkable incident of this kind occurred in the original band one cold winter night during the late 1930s. The late Walter Page, the bassist, had just had a new dental bridge made. His new teeth were so effective that he was able to eat a big barbecue dinner, after which he wrapped the ribs in some paper and threw them out the bus window.

The band had traveled another 75 miles before Page suddenly cried: "Hey, has anybody seen my teeth?" By that time, Jo Jones says, "it was too late and too cold to go back and find those teeth mixed up in those ribs. We just kept on going."

The shortest and best Basie story deals with Don Byas, the brilliant tenor saxophonist who played in the band for several months in 1941, and the beautifully tactful manner in which Byas quit the band on the usual two-weeks' notice basis.

The band was working at a theater and Basie was sitting quietly in his dressing room between shows, playing solitaire. Suddenly there was a sound. Basie looked up and saw Byas poke his head in the door.

"Basie?"

"What is it, Don?"

"In four weeks," said Byas, "I will have been gone two."

Whitey Mitchell: I have no trouble remembering the days when you could call up a certain super-hip New York disc jockey, ask for a Count Basie or a Prez record, and receive disdainful rebuke from on high for your trouble. It was the era of the Cool School, and it was definitely not In to be a Basie fan. Now that the Count is definitely In once more, this time, I hope, for good, this might be an appropriate time to recall an incident from the pre-*Well, All Right—April In Paris* days.

Count was working in a little gin mill in Albany with a seven piece combo. I came to town with the Shep Fields band to do a one-nighter, and when we had finished Rippling our Rhythm for the evening, some of us went over to hear Basie. No offense to his present crew, but I really enjoyed that combo more. The rhythm section did most of the playing, and that's the part of the Basie style that always killed me anyway. We stayed until the wee hours, in spite of the fact that we all had to get up early to leave for the next gig. As we were loading the cars in front of our hotel the next morning, we were surprised and delighted to see the Count himself come ambling out of the lobby.

He walked over to where our group was laboring to cram everything into the trunk, and struck up a conversation. He inquired about whose band we were, and recognized some of us as patrons of the previous evening. He told us about a disc jockey show he was to appear on as soon as he was sufficiently awake, and we promised to listen on the car radio. He was still standing there on the sidewalk rubbing his eyes as we waved and drove off.

As soon as we got clear of the streetcar and neon light interference, our driver turned on the radio. The first thing we heard was a Count Basie record from a strong local station. The disc jockey came on and announced that the great Count Basie was expected to be there in person any minute now, and would we please stay tuned. He sounded like kind of an idiot, but at least he was a Basie fan. We stayed tuned, unaccustomed to such good music on our one-nighters. The disc jockey broke into the music every few minutes to assure us that the great Count Basie would indeed be there IN PERSON any second now.

Finally, Count did arrive, and before he could even pull up into a comfortable chair, our friend the disc jockey launched into the most syntax-laden, double-talk-loaded, meaningless gibberish I've ever heard. It was in the form of a question, and though I couldn't possibly remember it from this one performance, I'll try to paraphrase it for you: "Count, wouldn't you say that, although jazz is primarily an American art form, having derived from Anglican sources certain tendencies which would, had they not, have been the influx of polytonal free forms, but perhaps should be ascribed to African concepts, if only through institutional therapy that circumscribes our view of syncopation, and that the beat, therefore, secondary only to improvisation, should be considered as having hitherto been relegated to what is germane, or rather what is intrinsic to so-called blue notes, and that this, then, could be considered more or less the secret of your success as a jazz artist?"

There was a pregnant pause as the Count evaluated this question, and then he replied, "No, I wouldn't say that."

By the time we got the car out of the ditch and got the radio working again, all we heard was recorded music, and, as far as I know, that was the full extent of the interview.

DAVE BRUBECK

In these days of State Department missions and triumphal world tours for the Dave Brubeck Quartet, it seems difficult to contemplate a Brubeck appearance that was a complete disaster.

The occasion was recalled by Mike Robbins in his notes for the album *Brubeck A La Mode* on Fantasy Records. For him, he said, Brubeck's name will always be associated with Jersey Joe Walcott.

"I had traveled deep into Philadelphia's ridge," he wrote, "the

Dave Brubeck

heart and possibly the lower colon of one of Philly's many Harlems." The scene, he added, was a club called the Blue Note, now defunct.

"The Blue Note was practically empty. A few couples smooched along the wall bench seats and perhaps a dozen others were scattered around the big rectangle bar . . ."

The Blue Note was so empty because this was the night of the Walcott-Marciano fight—the first one, in which the rapidly-aging Walcott was defending his newly-won title against the rampages of the Brockton Strong Boy.

"Dave played his first set, took his break and was halfway through the second when he was abruptly halted. Jack Fields, the old hand, big-band trumpet man who ran the Note, took the mike to chill the tiny crowd with the news that Marciano had just beaten Walcott, flattened him in the 13th round.

"If Jack had announced that Senator Eastland had mysteriously seized control of the White House, he couldn't have gotten a more gloomy or disheartening reaction. A groan, as if from one throat, rose from the audience. Dave started to play again, but it didn't help. Nothing would. Sullenly, the drinks were downed, change was snatched up, and one by one the people edged toward the door and out into the night, now grown cold . . . faces were grim as their owners contemplated the bets to be paid off on the morrow."

There was one more reason, perhaps equally important, why that particular evening was a low point of the Brubeck career. The fight took place at a time when, as Robbins pointed out, the quartet had just embarked on its first Eastern tour, and "hardly anyone had ever heard of this guy—what's his name?—Broback, Bluebeck, Broadbeak?

"It was back in 1952 B.T.C. (Before Time Cover)."

    ⋮

Paul Desmond, the eloquent and urbane alto saxophonist with Brubeck, spent several years trying to talk Dave, a teetotaler, into having a relaxing and friendly martini before dinner. Brubeck will now occasionally do so. Says Desmond, "Every five years or so, Dave makes a major breakthrough, like discovering room service."

    ⋮

14

In his Profile of Brubeck in *The New Yorker* Robert Rice wrote:

"In order to avoid congestion whenever they can, and get through it as painlessly as possible when they can't, the members of the quartet communicate with each other constantly while they are playing. Through such devices as hammering hard on a certain chord or rhythm for a bar or two, parodying each other's phrases, and (a favorite method of Desmond's) inserting explicit quotations from songs other than the one they are playing, they keep each other informed of their often conflicting views about the proper route to take or the progress they are making.

"Recently, at a college concert, a friend of Desmond's was in the audience, and during the intermission Desmond, who enjoys games, asked him to think of a number—any number—that could be worked into a saxophone solo. The friend proposed *Try A Little Tenderness.* He thought Desmond's assent to the request was slightly morose, but he simply supposed that the tune wasn't one of Desmond's favorites, and he was gratified to hear the saxophonist skillfully insert a long and lyrical excerpt from it into, surprisingly, the nine-eight number—a Brubeck composition whose name and nature is *Blue Rondo a la Turk.*

"What he wasn't cute enough to observe was that each of the other players, as soon as he heard what Desmond was doing, thought that he himself was being entreated to be tender. (The bassist) listened with increased attention to the sounds that were coming from his bass, but since they were the same ones he usually made, he kept right on making them. (The drummer) . . . courteously became more subdued—though *Blue Rondo* is, by design, a noisy number.

"Brubeck, strong in the consciousness of his own rectitude, retorted with a loud burst from *You're Driving Me Crazy—What Did I Do?*

"None of them were really appeased by Desmond's explanation, at the end of the concert, that he was only doing it for a friend."

Dizzy Gillespie

DIZZY GILLESPIE *by Patricia Willard*

It was 2 a.m. on a warm night in Los Angeles in 1950. John Birks Gillespie carefully took his horn apart, placed it in its case and made his way from the stand to a large ringside table of his acquaintances in the Club Oasis. "We're all going to Mexico this morning," he announced matter of factly.

Claims of prior commitments and all other attempts at declination of Dizzy Gillespie's characteristically declarative invitation were charmingly dismissed by him as he supervised the seating arrangement in a packed Cadillac which, not very many minutes later, was headed for the border.

A longtime frequent visitor to Southern California, Diz watched the nocturnal scenery, inquired about landmarks and tripled as navigator, wide-eyed tourist and academic researcher every minute. The first stop he ordered was at San Juan Capistrano. He peered intently at the dark skies, then shepherded his party into an all-night coffee shop where he politely demanded of the manager, "Where are the swallows?"

"Not till October 23rd," the man replied automatically. He did a double-take and shook his head violently as he looked up at the elegant pre-dawn group in nightclub attire filing out behind Diz, who solemnly nodded his acceptance of the data supplied.

"Oranges . . . real oranges growing on trees! Now I know I'm in California," our leader exclaimed with almost childish exuberance. Warning signs about illegal fruit picking ignored, Diz leaped from the car and speedily disappeared in the vast grove. Fifteen minutes later, the driver returned bewilderedly from his Gillespie-quest followed at a stealthy distance by Dizzy Gillespie leading at rope's length an even more bewildered-looking donkey, with whom Diz was attempting to share the armload of real oranges he had gathered from the trees that they were actually growing on.

In Tijuana, our tour director asked to be excused briefly to make a purchase in a store. He did not come back. The store-

17

keeper spoke no English and could give no clue as to the whereabouts of his recent customer. We slowly toured every street in the downtown section until we spotted enormous pink balloons drifting out of a burlesque establishment, blocks from where Diz had taken leave of us. Diz appeared a few minutes later carrying five more balloons, chuckling, "Y'know, these strippers in Mexico don't wear anything but balloons!"

At seven o'clock in the morning at the Club Los Angeles in Tijuana, Mexico, the drooping eyelids and lagging rhythms of the marimba house band were dreary testimony to the long hours the men had been playing. Obviously, the sounds offended Birks' spirited musical standards. After ordering what he called "breakfast" and what turned out to be a double shot of scotch for each of his famished guests, he slipped up the stairs to the catwalk-balcony supporting the instruments, snatched a pair of mallets and turned loose with what may have been the first marimba bop ever presented publicly. The renascence of the resident musicians was almost instantaneous, and the ensemble concert which ensued was probably one of the most outstanding inspirational performances Dizzy Gillespie has ever sparked.

Diz' destination, it turned out, was Rosarita Beach. He'd heard about it, and that's where he wanted to take his friends. En route, a gaunt, ragged *vaquero* with an ancient, weatherbeaten face was slumped on the bare back of a ribby old nag as he herded about a hundred cows to feed on the sparse growth beside the narrow highway.

Another command to halt.

South Carolina-born, sophisticated, urban, multi-lingual New Yorker and world traveler Gillespie had always been curious about what it felt like to be a cowboy. A brief exchange of words which must have been in Spanish because the elderly horseman seemed not at all uncomprehending as he turned his mount over to the stranger. Dizzy Gillespie, with neither saddle nor reins, dug in with his heels and at a gallop, circled the complacent cattle several times until he had them moving in the direction of a hilltop half a mile distant. There, he left them—and the horse—hiked back to the old man, to whom he presented a handful of U.S. dollars and waved him an "Adios" as he sped away in the Cadillac.

Diz discovered the mildly noisy delight of popping bulbous seaweed pods in the surf at Rosarita, where he led, or perhaps herded, his company of men with rolled up pants legs and barefoot women in cocktail dresses into the water for a mass mambo lesson. With great strings of dripping kelp draped around his shoulders, he danced, accenting the beats with a sharply squashed pod.

Back in Tijuana, Birks went on a shopping spree, maintaining he had no intention of being an exception to the souvenir-laden image of the U.S. tourist. His first purchase was a brilliantly multicolored sombrero whose fluted soft straw brim was six feet in diameter. Customarily, such hats are worn with the front turned back and flaring to the sides in a kind of inverted fan-shape.

Diz' flirtation with conformity was brief. He set out along the main street with the brim down all the way around, ruffling and fluttering about his knees. The spectacle of the gigantically gaudy hat with the stubs of legs propelling it froze dozens of passersby in speechless amazement until he entered a jewelry store, extended both arms just high enough to raise the flowing extremities of his headgear to display-counter level and began inquiring of the clerk in Spanish about prices of bracelets and brooches.

A middle-aged American (U.S.) woman in the front of the shop watched the scene. Suddenly, she clutched at her husband's arm and rasped, "Henry, look! Is *that* one of those *Mexicans?*"

Diz' preoccupation with distinctive hats has intensified. Knowing this, the wife of one of the musicians on a fairly recent recording session in Hollywood made him one of mink (which he wore all evening in the studio) because she had seen his enthusiasm at the Monterey Jazz Festival for the personally handwoven one presented him there by the wife of the local police chief. That lady, in turn, was responding to the pride she saw him display in the velvet and bejeweled African tarboosh he wore on stage with his voluminous blue and white striped robes and spiral-toed, openwork leather shoes.

A reporter at the Festival asked Diz about the origin of the costume and was rapidly scribbling the reply: "The robes," he explained, "are Nigerian. The shoes were crafted in Yugoslavia.

You see, I dig miscegenation." The writer gasped as Diz collapsed laughing at his interrogator's shock, then called for "Next question."

When so attired, Birks is often inclined to lecture proudly about his descendance from an African tribal chief who, he once confided, is actually an ancestor of his wife, Lorraine. Whatever the genealogy, Diz had a particularly favorite identity he enjoys assuming—Prince Iwo.

In February of 1963 he staged a quick private rehearsal with three members of his quintet in Portland, Oregon. They were not practicing the charts they would be playing the next night at the Black Hawk in San Francisco. They were preparing for the flight there.

Tall, dark, West Indian bassist Chris White; the considerably shorter and usually smiling drummer Rudy Collins, and shy, slender, mustachioed pianist Kenny Barron were dressed identically in dignified black suits and countenances so deadpan as to be virtually expressionless when they enplaned with His Highness. As per the preliminary runthrough, Chris, Rudy and Kenny maintained a respectful three-abreast distance of two steps to the rear and two to the left of their potentate except when approaching a doorway or a great many people. On these occasions, the leader paused while the rhythm section opened the door or cleared a passage for him to proceed while they stood at attention.

Diplomatic—and music business—protocol was observed on the plane. Prince Iwo traveled first class. His sidemen were in the coach section. None of them spoke.

At San Francisco International Airport, the artists resumed their places for the finale. Midafternoon crowds in the busy terminal clustered and gaped, wondering to each other in loud whispers about the identity of the entourage of the man in the robes. Prince Iwo stared even more intently at the commoners as though he could not believe that people could look like this. He commenced chattering in an unintelligible dialect with his attendants. They conferred in an equally unintelligible gibberish liberally laced with "Ungawas" as they, too, studied their audience.

Finally, a lone man approached the group determinedly,

pointed his finger at Diz' midsection and demanded, "Just what is that you're wearing?"

His Majesty turned to his subjects bewilderedly for a translation of their accoster's strange tongue. Again, they replied incoherently. A look of enlightenment, then indignation crossed Diz' face. "These are *my* clothes!" he announced emphatically in perfectly enunciated English, and the company marched off in formation to the taxi stand.

To their white cabby, they presented a slip of paper bearing the name of the hotel where they held reservations and proceeded into a violent and extended argument among themselves in pseudo-African double talk all the way there. The driver began to show signs of nervous uneasiness. At the hotel, the passengers looked uncomprehendingly when the fare was quoted. Everybody "Ungawa"-ed. The cabby began raising his voice and pointing to the meter. The passengers got more excited and more confused. In desperation, the man held up eight fingers and slowly counted them to indicate the dollars owed.

"Man, why didn't you say so in the first place?" Diz smiled warmly as he handed him a ten dollar denomination in United States currency and gestured that no change was necessary.

Dizzy Gillespie's refreshingly uninhibited wit is not always employed in putting other people on. He is equally quick to punctuate an earnest and knowledgeable discussion of international affairs with devastatingly ironic and original satiric observations or to tell a funny story on himself.

When he spoke to an auditorium full of University of California students across the street from the Berkeley campus he recounted what he called one of his most embarrassing experiences. He had telephoned the office of a highly recommended Negro dermatologist in Seattle for an appointment. The receptionist asked the nature of his difficulty. "I'm turning white!" he exclaimed, and laughed. He thought it was a good joke and was disappointed at not hearing at least a giggle from her. The next day the receptionist greeted him at the doctor's office. "She was a white girl," he said dismally.

No encounter with Dizzy Gillespie on or off the stage is ever without both musical and verbal humor as well as intense virtuoso seriousness. Some of his nightclub dissertations, however, have become such classics that he dare not abandon them—like his explanation at the beginning of a set: "I'm sorry we're a little late getting started this evening, but you see, we just came from a very, very important show. The Ku Klux Klan and the John Birch Society were giving a benefit for the Catholic Youth Organization and the B'Nai Brith. It was held at the Harlem YMCA . . . so you can see we're very lucky to be here at *all* this evening."

Some are so popular he constantly embellishes them, abetted hilariously in the past couple of years by the irrepressibly extemporaneous talents of Chris White, who shares with Birks the rare twin gifts of perfect timing in both his musical inventiveness and his delivery of a laugh-getting line. Diz has been bringing down the house for nearly a decade with his "And now I'd like to introduce the members of the band," at which point every man on the stand turns and shakes hands and exchanges names with his fellow musicians. The routine now goes more than five minutes with Chris shouting "God Save The Queen" in response to the announcement of his West Indies homeland, donning a white handkerchief over his face as Rudy Collins forms a cross with his drumsticks at a reference to "Havana, Mississippi," minueting with Diz and looking beautifully indignant when Diz refuses to believe Chris' surname.

More and more of Birks' contemporary performances are becoming cooperative projects with the quintet. In 1961, at Newport, Rhode Island, the group stopped for breakfast after the Festival at a pancake house unfortunately called "Sambo's." Diz asked the waitress how she liked working for Mr. Sambo. She said she liked it fine, thank you. Chris asked her what Sambo's *first* name was. She said she didn't know. Leo Wright expressed a desire to meet Mr. Sambo so he could find out his first name for himself. She said he wasn't in. Rudy thought maybe it was a Mr. Sambo he met once and asked her to describe him. She couldn't and finally blurted out that she had never met him and didn't really know if there was a Mr. Sambo. Argentine pianist Lalo Schifrin came to her rescue, insisting that there must be a Mr. Sambo—how else would the place get a name like that?—and he'd be willing to bet it was the same Pascuale Sambo he used to know back home in Buenos Aires. The girl shot Lalo a look of intense gratitude and fled to the kitchen.

At several spots around the country, the Dizzy Gillespie For President movement, originally a promotion gimmick of the forties, is springing up again. In 1963, the Southern California contingent of Gillespie constituents gathered at a party in his honor in the swank Benedict Canyon section of staid Beverly Hills. There is still conjecture as to precisely what caused the traffic jam of Cadillacs, Lincolns and Rolls Royces in front of the house where the party was being held.

There was this very well illuminated sign six feet high and fourteen feet long stretched across the front porch . . . so it could have been the two-foot-high letters announcing "Dizzy Gillespie For President Rally Tonight" or it could have been the line beneath it saying the event was under the auspices of an organization Leonard Feather founded—The John Birks Society!

The aura of good fun and serio-comic hero worship that has surrounded John Birks through the years has given rise to dozens of stories like those detailed above, yet his admirers have never lost sight of the central fact of the Gillespie legend: his extraordinary musical contribution. The anecdotes may cling to him forever but his position as a founder of modern jazz will never be obscured.

Even on this subject, though, Diz is often inclined to take a humorously evasive position. Perhaps a significant key to his personality can be found in his reaction to one of those inevitable arguments concerning the respective roles of Diz and Charlie Parker in the development of the new music.

Asked who he thought was really the prime mover in the bebop revolution, Dizzy retorted: "I'd like to answer that by asking another question. What is the most important ingredient in spaghetti sauce?"

BENNY GOODMAN

Benny Goodman has earned a threefold niche as a jazz celebrity. His importance and influence as a clarinetist have been a matter of record since the 1920s; his pioneer part in establishing the big jazz band as a commercial popular entity was acknowledged in the mid-1930s. At the same time, Goodman earned the gratitude of the music world when, by hiring Teddy Wilson, then Lionel Hampton and others, he made the first firm steps in the elimination of Jim Crow in jazz.

A fourth side of B.G. is less known outside the profession, though it has been the subject of discussion among musicians since he first came to prominence. Benny's superb musicianship, like that of many other artists, has always involved such intense dedication that it has often seemed difficult for him to concentrate for any great length of time on other subjects. As a consequence, his absentmindedness has given rise to many anecdotes.

One of the best known Goodman stories, recalled by Peggy Lee, concerns the time when he and Peggy jumped into a taxicab outside the RCA Building. Awaiting instructions, the driver reamined motionless while Benny just sat there quietly for several minutes. Finally the driver said, "Well, buddy?"

Benny looked up with a start, said: "Ah, how much is that?" and fished for his wallet as he started to get out of the cab.

•

Artie Shaw tells a story of the days when both he and Benny were working in a New York radio studio orchestra. At the time Artie was spending every spare moment engrossed in a book. One day during rehearsal Benny walked in and, glancing at him with a grin, offered a greeting: "Hello, J.B." The next day there was a similar encounter as Benny waved to him and called out: "Hiya, J.B." This went on for several days until Shaw could contain his curiosity no longer. "What do you mean with all this J.B. business." "Why," Goodman said, "Judge Bernard Shaw."

•

One habit for which Benny is well remembered by former side-men was his tendency to borrow clarinet reeds from members of his sax section. Though the saxophonists rarely needed them, since there was not much music in the book that called for them to double on clarinet, occasional situations arose that made Good-man's borrowing proclivity a little confusing. One night, after Goodman had borrowed Vido Musso's last clarinet reed, he called a tune called *Bach Goes To Town,* the only number that featured a five-clarinet passage.

"I can't play it, Benny," said Musso.

"Why not?"

"No reed."

"Then," said Goodman with an air of finality, "fake it!"

•

On a train trip once, Benny went into the diner alone, sat down, and began to look at a new score. The car was crowded and it was some time before the waiter arrived.

Placing the order card in front of Benny to fill out, the waiter stood there expectantly. Benny suddenly looked up, rather startled, then signed the card and walked away.

André Previn: One day a few years ago Benny came to hear my trio at the Roundtable in New York. He wanted us to record with him, and he said he'd like us to be at his house in Connecticut for rehearsal. "It's going to be a busy day," he said, "so I'd like you to be there at nine in the morning."

"But Benny," I said, "we work here at the Roundtable until four in the morning."

Benny had a perfect solution for that. He suggested, "You be sure to go home right after the job tonight."

:

During rehearsal we had a lot of trouble, because it was a bit-terly cold day and our fingers were practically numb. Helen Ward, who was Benny's original vocalist years ago, was back with him for this record date, and she finally said:

25

"Benny, you know what the trouble is? It's just horribly cold in here."

"You know," said Benny, "you're absolutely right." And he promptly put on a warm woolen sweater and resumed rehearsing.

:

In 1962 Benny's band played an engagement at Disneyland. At that time he had Whitey Mitchell playing bass with him. Well, Whitey's brother Red went to visit him there. Whitey and Red are the same size so, for a gag, just to put Benny on, between sets they switched clothes, and Red put on Whitey's uniform.

Red went on the bandstand and started to play a set. During the set Benny took a glance at him several times and didn't say anything. They finished the set and Benny said: "Aren't you *Red* Mitchell?" And Red said: "Yes."

Benny never did say anything, but Red could imagine him saying to himself: "That's funny. I could have sworn I had Whitey on the band."

Whitey Mitchell: Sonny Igoe, the drummer, recalls an incident from his pre-CBS days when he was playing drums with the King of Swing. They were appearing at the Paramount Theater on Broadway, and this was Benny's first and last venture into the big band be-bop field. As they were waiting to go into the pit one day, Sonny mentioned to Benny that as a child of twelve he had stood in line for three hours at that same theater to hear the great Goodman band of that day. Benny seemed a little surprised to hear this, and inquired, "Well, why didn't you come backstage, Pops?"

•

Goodman at times can even be absentminded about his absentmindedness. Once at the Hollywood Bowl he was leading a combo that included André Previn, Red Mitchell, and Red Norvo. During the applause after one tune he walked over to Norvo and softly hummed a tune. "What's that thing called?"

"That's *Sunny Side Of The Street,*" said Norvo.

Benny then walked back to the microphone and announced the tune to the audience. While the band was playing the introduction he ambled back to Norvo. "How does it go? Hum me the first four bars."

.

Benny is not always realistic about financial matters. When Terry Gibbs was very young and impecunious, Benny once visited his apartment and, commenting on its sleaziness, offered to find him a place. A couple of days later he called up. "Terry, I've found you a place. Real nice." It turned out the rent was $500 a month. At that time Gibbs' entire income consisted of $75 a week from a television show with Goodman.

It is Gibbs who tells what is perhaps the definitive Goodman story, one that is quite literally without a punchline.

Gibbs was telling Goodman one of his typical musicians' jokes. Goodman stood listening, apparently fascinated. Terry was just about to reach what was obviously going to be the punchline— when Goodman turned on his heels and walked away.

Charlie Barnet: Benny Goodman at the Paramount had on the bill with him an ace dancing act, the Condos Brothers, Nick and Steve, also the Ink Spots.

Benny, as was customary, played the first number, then the girl singer came out and sang her couple of songs. She got off, and now it was time for the first act.

Benny got up there, and he had obviously forgotten the name of the act. He says, "Now, folks, uh, uh, here are the Ink Brothers."

The Condos Brothers came wailing out, did a fast number, and as they finished Nick turned and said, "Thank you, Tommy Dorsey!"

Ed Kelly: When Artie Shaw had his band at the Lexington Hotel, Benny used to go to hear him on his off-nights from the Cafe Rouge. One night Artie is playing, and has all those strings behind him and everything, and Benny dances past the front of the bandstand. He looks at Artie and says, "You know, if you had glasses, you'd look like Benny Goodman."

So Artie says, "Yeah, and if you could play clarinet they'd call you Artie Shaw."

Carlos Gastel: When Harry James and Ziggy Elman were both in Benny's band, Benny of course was impressed with both of them. This, however, left poor Chris Griffin with nothing to do but play in the section—no solos. Finally Chris told Leonard Vannerson, the road manager, that he was turning in his notice.

Well, after the job that night, Leonard was riding with Benny in Goodman's car and didn't know how to tell him about Chris, because Benny liked Griffin a great deal. So they pulled up to a diner and Leonard said, "Benny, Chris gave me his notice." Benny didn't say anything, just kept quiet and walked into the diner. He ordered some scrambled eggs.

When they came, he took the ketchup bottle and the top fell off, right in the middle of the eggs. Well, Benny was so preoccupied he ate all around the bottle top, without moving it. Finally there's nothing left of the eggs but the part that's under the top.

They get back in the car and Leonard starts driving again, and now it's about five o'clock in the morning. A farmer's milk truck pulls out of a side road abruptly and the car ran right into it. Leonard jams on the brakes, there's milk all over the street, the horse that was pulling the wagon is making an awful racket, and the farmer is screaming. Finally Benny broke his long silence.

He said, "Now what did Chris want to do a thing like that for?"

VIDO MUSSO

One of the most popular jazz figures of the 1940s was Vido Musso, who won three of the annual *Down Beat* readers' polls as the foremost sideman tenor saxophonist.

Musso in recent years has been working successfully as leader of his own combo in Las Vegas. He is said also to have done very well financially through canny dealings in real estate. But possibly the best known of all his accomplishments is his unique approach to the English language.

Born in Carrini, Sicily, Vido came to the United States at the age of seven. Though he was educated for the next ten years in

Detroit and subsequently moved to Los Angeles, his origin has remained an essential in his personality. He is regarded as fondly by musicians as Yogi Berra is by ballplayers.

One of the best known stories about Vido goes back to a period not long before Pearl Harbor when he was a member of the Harry James orchestra, which had been booked by the Music Corporation of America for a tour of Canada.

Members of the band rehearsed Vido for his declaration as the bus approached the border, for Canada was already at war with Italy. "Be cool about it," they said. "If the immigration man asks where you were born, just say New York City."

Vido proceeded to take a nap. The next thing he remembered was the tap of an official on his shoulder, as the officers entered the bus at the crossing point, and the sound of a voice saying "Where were you born?"

Still half-asleep, Vido mumbled: "Sicily. Where else?"

Then, suddenly aware that he had created a situation, he hastily added: "You don't have to worry about a thing. M.C.A. straightened it all out so I could come in."

"M.C.A.? What's that?" asked the inspector.

Vido's reaction was a mixture of indignation and incredulity. "Hey, Harry, come here," he cried. "This dumb s.o.b. doesn't know what M.C.A. is!"

And that was how Vido lost his place on the bus.

On another occasion Vido's combo was working in a San Francisco club opposite Georgie Auld's group when Auld accidentally caught sight of a letter to Vido from Mrs. Musso, signed "Yours truly, Rose."

"Hey, Vido," he said, "how come you've been married all these years and she says yours truly?"

"Don't let that throw you," Vido assured him, "we're very attacked to each other."

One night in the band bus during Vido's years in the Benny Goodman band there were clouds of cigaret smoke in the air. Vido became alarmed.

"Somebody open the window," he implored, "or we'll all get sophisticated!"

Vido's ability to read music in those days was limited, as Benny Goodman found out soon after hiring him in 1936. After a preliminary rehearsal by the saxophone section it became clear that there might be some difficulty in a band that relied as heavily as Goodman's on clean, accurately-read performances.

"What seems to be the trouble, Vido?" Benny asked.

"It's not the notes I can't read, Benny," came the answer. "It's the rest-ess."

Soon after, Vido appeared at rehearsal with a severe boil on his neck. A day or two later it had disappeared, for, as Vido explained, "I had it glanced, and the doctor put some easy tape over it."

Clarinetist Gus Bivona recalls several typical Mussoisms. Looking out of a bus window, Vido pointed to some fields and said, "Geez, look at all the cotton on those sheeps."

Watching an underseas picture, he remarked, "Boy, those octopuses put their technicals around you just like a boa constructor."

Once, when Vido was playing a society date, a lady requested a tango. And Vido, the great boulevardier, said, "Certainly, madame," and he turned around and asked the guys about tangos. They picked one out to fake; Vido got ready to count it off, and said, "Okay, here we go. ONE! twoTHREE! FOUR!

On one of those long bus trips, some of the men would play word games to break the boredom. One of them called for a man to give the initials of a bandleader he was thinking of and the others would try to guess who it was.

Then it came to Vido.

"E.C.," he said.

The men kept coming up with names like Eddie Condon and Emil Coleman, but Vido just kept shaking his head. Finally they gave up. "Who are you thinking of?" they asked.

"Ex-avier Cugat," said Vido.

WINGY MANONE

Born around Mardi Gras time in New Orleans in 1904, Wingy Manone was given his first trumpet in 1912. He lost his right arm in 1914, the most meaningful of all the dates in relation to most of the anecdotes about him.

On one occasion he received a birthday present from Joe Venuti, a large, elaborately wrapped box. After spending fifteen minutes opening it, Wingy discovered that it contained a single cuff link.

Zeke Zarchy recalls the time when Wingy had a sore throat and was about to make a record date. A doctor prescribed some pills and Wingy went into training, determined that on this occasion he would be less instead of more guttural than usual.

After the first take the recording director came rushing into the studio in a state of panic. "Who do you think you are," he cried, "Bing Crosby?" Wingy had refined his voice to the point of ruin. It took two packs of cigarets and a fifth of whiskey to restore the real Manone sound.

Once when Wingy had to play an engagement in Chicago during one of the city's worst snowstorms, he went to a store to buy a glove.

The clerk insisted that he sold gloves only by the pair.

Wingy insisted that he had no need of a pair of gloves; all he wanted was one glove.

After considerable argument, the clerk won and sold him a pair of gloves. The package was paid for and wrapped when Wingy, just before walking out with it, turned around, looked over his shoulder at the clerk and said:

"You guys in Chicago sure give it to the tourists, don't you?"

In his autobiography, *Trumpet On The Wing,* Manone told of a joke played on him by Eddie Connors, owner of the Somerset Club in San Antonio, Texas.

For a booking at the club Wingy picked up a guitarist named

Snoozer Quinn, of whom he says: "Snoozer had only one eye, but he could play a mess of guitar, and nobody ever paid any attention to his lamps. However, in the same band there was "Hooknose," Joe Loyocano, with a cork leg, and me with one wing, and a few other cats with parts missing. Altogether, I had nine men.

"At the end of the week I went to get paid, and Connors handed me the dough. I counted the money, and there was a man short. I got paid for only eight instead of nine.

" 'Where do you get that jive?' I asked Connors . . .

"Then he told me: 'Look around . . . Among the nine of you, there's a whole man missin'. Here's your salary for eight men.' "

Wingy also wrote about the time when his friend Bing Crosby's house burned down. As Crosby and Manone dug around in the ruins, they came across one clothes closet that had been only partly demolished. Bing had a variety of sports coats hanging in the closet; the fire had only reached one side of them, burning off the right arm of each jacket.

"Hey man," cried Wingy, "these are for me!"

Arty Stein, recalls Shorty Sherock, was a real character who at one time played in Wingy's band. They were always kidding each other, and one night Wingy said to him: "Man, you're the worst drummer in the world."

"What makes you so sure?" said Stein.

"You're working for *me*," said Wingy.

The parting of the ways inevitably arrived and Wingy decided it would be advisable to make the separation as formal and legal as possible. Instead of telling Stein he was through, he gave him a written, carefully worded two weeks' notice, which Stein received just a couple of days before Christmas.

Arty looked at the document and turned to Wingy, crestfallen.

"Well, what's the matter?" said Wingy. "It's worded right, ain't it?"

"Sure," said Stein, "but Wingy . . . at this time of year, the least you could do was gift-wrap it."

EDDIE CONDON

Eddie Condon has three reputations: as alcohol's bottomless cup, as jazz's literary wit, and as guitarist.

Condon's cure for a hangover has been widely quoted: comedians in Las Vegas have been heard to use it without crediting the source—"Take the juice of two quarts of whiskey. . . ."

Condon's liquid intake led to two serious attacks of pancreatitis. In his book, *Eddie Condon's Treasury of Jazz*, co-authored by Richard Gehman, it was recalled that he was given up for dead both times, and that doctors warned him his next drink would be his last. His reaction was typically Condonian: "I changed doctors."

Close to death from one of the attacks, Condon was being given a whiskey enema. Weakly he looked at the doctor and whispered, "Doc, see what the rest of the boys on the ward will have."

Gehman also says this of Eddie:

"Much of his conversation is couched in this kind of understatement. One morning after the saloon closed I drove him to New Jersey. It began to rain as we started out. At Linden, New Jersey, we had to stop for a red light. The Esso refineries are located there, and the ugly silver tanks sit like enormous tombstones in the stinking marshes. The air is continually smoky and sooty, the gray sky seems to blend with the brown desolation of the landscape, and by the roadside are several old workmen's shacks plastered with windtorn circus and movie posters. As we were waiting for the light to change, Condon surveyed this scene with interest.

"Phyllis and I have been thinking of buying out here," he said.

And there was the time that a man once mentioned to Condon that he was sitting home having "a delicious drink of whiskey."

"What did you put in it to make it taste that way?" asked Condon.

One evening, George Frazier remembers, when Condon was at a party where some Eddy Duchin piano solos were being played on the phonograph, a gushing girl approached him and said: "Don't you simply adore Eddy Duchin, Mr. Condon? What I mean is, he really makes the piano talk, don't you think?"

Condon raised an eyebrow, jerked his head back as if he were ducking away from an uppercut, and said, "He certainly does. The piano says, 'Please take your clumsy hands off me.' "

Though most of his quips have been delivered in person, at Dixieland concerts, at his house in Greenwich Village or at the club that bears his name, Condon has collaborated with Gehman on a series of literary ventures. One of the most fruitful was a weekly series of newspaper columns inaugurated in 1954 for the *New York Journal-American*, in which he became a record critic.

Most of the items he elected to review were popular rather than jazz records. Not surprisingly, the brickbats outnumbered the bouquets by about ten to one. A few of them:

Of *The Thundisbreak*, by the Sauter-Finegan Orchestra: "This is the Sauteed-Fingers version of the old John Philip Sousa march, *The Thunderer*. Personally I'd rather listen to real thunder. Music of this kind ought to be played close to elephants. The other side, *Science Fiction* . . . has all the intimacy of a death sentence."

Of an item by Hugo Winterhalter: "I put on *The Little Shoe-maker*. I took it right off again, too. The most distressing thing about it is that it's current. I can't face the thought of going through a revival of it in a couple of years."

Of Vaughn Monroe's *Mr. Sandman:* A better name for this would be *Mr. Sandthroat* . . . I hear this is a comeback for Monroe, and I can't help wondering if this trip was really necessary."

His reaction to the tremulous voice of Eartha Kitt was summed up in one succinct phrase: "She sounds as though she was recording during a stickup."

About the trend toward echo-chamber recording and electronic instruments, he commented: "These days you can't be a singer unless you operate in a wind tunnel, or death chamber, or whatever it is they call those caves over at the recording studios . . . and you can't be a musician unless you've got four or five electric cords trailing off your instrument and two more plugged into your ears."

Of the singing voice of Sammy Davis, Jr. he observed: "He sounds like Nat King Cole has joined the Marines."

Of a new release by Arthur Godfrey: "This *must* be National Hog Calling Week. But I tell you, I don't want Arthur calling any of *my* hogs."

Condon expressed mock horror when the Boston Pops Orchestra under Arthur Fiedler came out with an arrangement by Robert Russell Bennett of *Look Sharp—Be Sharp,* the commercial TV jingle for Gillette: "This is the razor blade song, but in this arrangement it's almost too dull to listen to. This is the greatest argument I've ever heard in favor of electric shaves."

On one of the relatively rare occasions when he reviewed a modern jazz record—a Norman Granz jam session featuring such artists as Stan Getz, Wardell Gray, Benny Carter and Willie Smith —he wrote: "One saxophone solo reminded me of a dog, just poisoned by a neighbor, who goes up to another dog and says, 'Boy, oh boy, I've just had one hell of a meal!' "

But Eddie's definitive statement on modern jazz was made the night a waiter at the Condon Club dropped a trayload of dishes.

"Please, please," said Condon. "None of that modern stuff in here."

GEORGE SHEARING

(Unlike most blind performers, George Shearing is completely unself-conscious about his lack of sight. At one time his publicity agent sent out a story that arrangements had been made for Shearing to judge a beauty contest—using the Braille system. The following reminiscences are typical of the incidents in which he has been involved.)

I am always very flattered by people's realization and acceptance of the fact that I have some kind of sense of humor. Because of this, people are always playing gags on me. I like that.

Many years ago in England I had a drummer working with me by the name of Norman Burns. When we had meals together, he would cut up my food for me. Some times he would break up a slice of bread and spread bits of bread all over the top of the food and say, "I don't know, George, I hope you like what you have to-night, it looks kind of funny to me." Or perhaps he wouldn't say anything. And I'd dig into this thing and expect meat and potatoes.

One evening he prepared an even greater surprise for me. He put a menu over the top of everything. No matter how broad-minded you are in your tastes in food, I really can't recommend sliced menu.

One night Norman got me involved in a discussion with some-body else, and while I was preoccupied he slipped—unbeknownst to me, and this was pretty clever because I am usually kind of ob-servant when somebody does something to me—slipped a bunch of knives, forks and spoons in my coat pocket. When we left I paid the bill and the manager came over to say good night. He said, "George, I appreciate your patronage, but I can't help feeling it's a little cheap of you to take the cutlery out of the restaurant."

Another time my wife said to him, "Norman, I'm loaded with parcels; will you please take George." I think we were coming out of a basement broadcast studio. This was during the war, when they used to deliver huge piles of coal and dump them all over the place. Norman said, "George, we've got to go over this great big mound of coal here. This is the only way we can make it." So, while Trixie is climbing up a perfectly normal flight of stairs I'm climbing up this huge pile of coal and, before I realize what's happening, my face and clothes and everything are covered with the stuff. That one didn't seem very funny at the time.

When I was playing in London at a place called Hatchett's, there were a lot of gags going on. Fellows in the band knew I couldn't stand the smell of cheese, so they got the strongest cheese they could find and put it right plunk in front of me on the piano.

I don't know whether you've ever noticed it or not, but I have a tendency to rock back and forth while I'm playing, and the first time I went forward in Hatchett's that cheese really hit me. I couldn't play for about five minutes.

I guess I'm quite a prankster myself. One night somebody in the band—it was so long ago I can't quite remember but it may very well have been me—put garlic on the reeds and mouthpieces of all the guys' horns.

The bandleader gave the beat; he said, "Ready, fellows, one. . . . two. . . . three. . . . four. . . ." and all you heard was "Hmmph." Everybody had put their instruments to their mouths and started sneezing and coughing and gagging. Not a single note came out.

Trixie Shearing: Somebody came up to George once when our daughter Wendy was a baby and said, "George, it must be terrible, don't you want to know what your wife and baby look like?" and George said, "I know what they look like," and he does.

He came home one night from a night club and said to me, "You know, all this talk about Jane Russell's figure is grossly exaggerated."

I said, "What do you mean? How do you know?"

"Well," he said, "she came in the club and they invited me to sit down at the table and I put my arm out to shake hands and, after all, I'm blind, and I fumbled. Her figure's not that good."

George Shearing: Naturally, we have our own following, and I presume that since we are drawing a pretty fat salary for playing in a club we must be responsible for pulling in a large number of people. But, you wouldn't believe it, in quite a number of cases people come in and don't even know what band is playing.

Once while playing in a club I had a woman come over to the bandstand and say, "What's the name of this band? I like it." I figured I might as well play along with the gag so I said, "Irving Tishman." She said, "Are you Mr. Tishman?" "I am," I said. "Well I really enjoy your music, Mr. Tishman," she said. I played it dead straight and the next day when I woke up I had visions of this woman going all around New York asking for the latest releases by Irving Tishman.

This name, incidentally, was inspired by Bobby Sherwood, who always used to come to see us when we were at the Embers. He would always get himself a ringside table and announce himself to me by saying, "Shearing—Irving Tishman here."

There was another incident in San Francisco when we were playing at the Black Hawk. I don't know whether a bunch of hip people were putting this woman on or whether she just didn't hear my name right, but anyway she came up to me and said, "Mr. Gershwin, I really enjoy your music very much." I didn't want to embarrass her so I said, "Thank you very much indeed."

Later on she came back.

"Mr. Gershwin, it's me again. Sincerely, you bring tears to my eyes, Mr. Gershwin."

Finally I couldn't resist. At the end of the set I said to her, "I want to introduce you to my wife, Ira."

:

My wife and I have had a gimmick going for years: I tell people I can smell money.

If it's a one-dollar bill, she does nothing. If it's a five she taps me once, with the knee or the hand. If it's a ten, she taps twice, twenty three times, fifty four times.

Once we were sitting around in the Papagayo room in San Francisco, Jimmy Lyons, Nat Cole, June Christy, Billy Eckstine, Stan Kenton, Trixie and myself, and the subject of money came up.

Trixie said, "You know, of course, George can tell the denomination of money by smelling it."

So they were handing out bills and she was tapping; they said, "Well, you're giving him some kind of signal."

Trixie could see there was a one-dollar bill coming so she said, "All right, if you think I'm giving him any signals, I'll move over here," and went clean over to the other side of the table.

The money came out and I knew that because she was moving away, it was a one-dollar bill, so I smelled it and said, "It's a one."

Nat Cole said, "How do you do it?" and I said, "Nat, it's very simple; for different monetary denominations, they use different grades of ink. Each grade has its own peculiar smell." He shrugged his shoulders and said, "All right. If you don't want to tell me, that's all right." And he walked away.

Five years later I told him.

:

Once during the war, when they had the blackouts, the night time speed limit was 25 miles an hour. Trixie had to hurry to get me to a performance and, riding in the back of the car with us were Anne Shelton, a very famous English girl singer, and her father.

We were about halfway there when the father spoke up from the back and said, "I'm awfully sorry to tell you this, Trixie, but you're exceeding the speed limit."

"Oh, don't worry about that" said Trixie, "after all, where would I find a cop hanging around the street at this time of night?"

And he said "Right here, in the back seat. I'm one." And he was.

DUKE ELLINGTON

Duke Ellington's relationship with his public has always been marked by three key virtues: urbanity, mundanity, and lack of profanity. Never at a loss for the perfectly timed answer, he came up with a typical gem in 1958 when his band played at the outdoor music festival in Stonybrook, Long Island.

While they were playing *Such Sweet Thunder,* a small plane with a loud engine flew so low that it could not be ignored. Duke acknowledged it, gave a down beat, changed the tempo of the music to match the intruding sounds, and directed the plane along with the orchestra.

The audience applauded appreciatively and the master of ceremonies, Norman Brokenshire, said, "Duke, your command of the band is superb; but how did you arrange for that plane to come over at just the right time?"

Duke allowed a fittingly dramatic pause before replying suavely, "Well, Norman, we consider ourselves primitive artists; we employ the materials at hand."

:

In 1959 Duke was separated from his band for an unusually long period—six weeks—while he composed for and appeared in the film *Anatomy Of A Murder* on location at Ishpeming, Michigan. During a session at the Columbia recording studios on the night of his reunion with the men, Duke pointed to tenor saxophonist Paul Gonsalves, indicating that it was time for his solo on one of the *Anatomy* themes.

Paul protested that his music was blank at that spot.

"Ah, baby," said Duke with a typically gracious smile, "that's where you take over on the adlibsophone."

:

A constant source of irritation to Duke are the fans and "experts" who try to dictate to him what kind of music he should or should not write and play. When objections were raised to his doing such things as *Asphalt Jungle Twist* and *One More Twist,* he unburdened himself of a few observations:

"Why shouldn't Duke Ellington do *One More Twist?* Does anybody scream when Dizzy Gillespie twists? No; they respect him and his music and appreciate his humor. But me? There's so much prejudice against me. The rock 'n' roll industry was built on my music. Al Sears and Jimmy Forrest came right out of my band with my music in their pockets, and they did all right. But let Duke Ellington play *One More Twist* and everybody screams, 'That's not music . . . that's not jazz . . . that's not Ellington!'

"This is plain race prejudice—*my* race! I'm the only one in my race, you understand. I'm all alone, and alone I have to face this terrible prejudice against me. Nobody suffers from prejudice like I suffer from Ellington prejudice!"

Joe Morgen: In 1950 David K. Niles, an administrative assistant to President Truman, expressed interest in having Duke Ellington pay a visit to the White House. The idea was for Duke to present

Duke Ellington

Mr. Truman with the manuscript of *Harlem,* an important new work he'd written.

Duke kept brushing the whole thing aside, saying "What would I do there?" and pretending he wasn't going; but he was finally finessed into it. The band was playing the Howard Theater in Washington, closing there on a Thursday night, and Duke was supposed to meet Mr. Truman the next morning.

Suddenly, late Thursday, a new problem arose. Okay, he said, he would go to the White House, but he had nothing suitable to wear!

There was only one thing for me to do: I had to take the sleeper to New York, try to get into his apartment, pick out some clothes, take the train back and get them to him first thing in the morning.

Well, I got to New York and there was nobody in the apartment and I had no key; and when I finally got hold of Willie, Duke's valet, he refused to let me in. He didn't know about any Presidents and he didn't want any part of such nefarious goings-on.

I forget exactly what threats I used, but I used language I wouldn't have used even in front of HST. "You'd better be waiting in front of that apartment in 15 minutes," I told him on the phone, "or I'll break your ——" I can't remember the rest of it, but anyhow, I hung up, went to Duke's apartment, and there was Willie.

While I went through Duke's clothes closets he stood there warning me of all the dire consequences that could spell disaster for both of us. Then I got together with Mr. John Popkin, owner of the Hickory House, where Duke has his dinners when he's in New York. Mr. Popkin picked out about ten blue ribbon steaks to take along—for Truman, not Ellington—and we dashed to the train and got back to Washington about 6 a.m.

At 10 a.m. I received a call that Duke was due at the White House at 12:10 p.m. I called the little hotel across the street from the theater to wake Duke up.

"Duke Ellington?" the operator said. "He's not here. The whole band left last night."

I got dressed in about eight seconds, dashed into a taxi and over to the hotel. "What room *was* he in?" I asked.

"Room 2."

I went to Room 2 and banged on the door as if it was the last chance to get out of the hotel alive. No answer. I had just turned to walk away when the door opened slowly and a man who looked like a sleep-walker looked at me blankly.

"Duke!" I said. "For God's sake, it's almost eleven and you're due at the White Hous in an hour! Let me help you get ready!"

"No," said Duke, yawning. "If you stay here it will only slow me up. You go ahead and I'll meet you there."

"No, no; I'm laying out your clothes!"

"The longer you stay, the longer I'll be in bed."

"Duke, do you realize the importance of this meeting? And you still have to shower and shave and get dressed, and then—"

"Listen, Joe," said Duke, "I was born in this city, and I know one thing for sure: you can get *anywhere* in Washington in ten minutes. Now go on, Joe. I'll see you at the White House."

I gave in.

At the specified entrance on Pennsylvania Avenue, with Popkin, I asked whether they had the names of Ellington, Morgen and Popkin on the list for admission.

"Ellington, yes; Morgen, Popkin, no."

That was the least of our problems. Watching our watches was the worst. 11:45, and no Duke. Noon, and still no Duke. Five after, and I was in no condition to meet anybody but my Maker.

At exactly 12:08½ p.m. a big Chrysler limousine drew up, with Henry Snodgrass at the wheel. Out stepped Edward K., fresh as a lily, shaved, groomed, immaculate, looking like a Secretary of State.

Oh yes, they let us all in. We went into the rotunda, and a protocol officer called us, and there was Harry S. Truman sitting with a press secretary. The President jumped to his feet. Duke walked toward him, very erect, very elegant, and bowed a deep bow.

"Hiya, Duke!" said the President.

"How do you do, Mr. President," said Duke. "You know, I've come in behalf of the kids on the corner who couldn't get into a place like this."

That seemed to strike just the right note, and the ten minutes

Duke was supposed to be alone with the President turned out to stretch into twenty-five.

This was during the very critical time when the Berlin airlift was on. Madame Pandit and several Ambassadors who had appointments with the President were kept waiting while the two piano players were chatting.

Finally Duke came out, and immediately he was surrounded by a swarm of photographers and reporters. A white Southern correspondent asked in a mocking, condescending manner, like "Well now Duke, how you-all find the President of the United States to be?"

Nothing fazed Duke, of course. Without batting an eyelash, he said very gently:

"Oh, I found him just as I would expect my family doctor to be—very reassuring."

I'll bet he couldn't have been any more reassured than I'd been at exactly 12:08½ p.m. that afternoon.

P.S. I also had all kinds of difficulty getting Duke to agree to be the guest of honor at the National Press Club. He was the first Negro ever to appear there. By the time he was through, he had everybody from Drew Pearson to Arthur Krock keeping time to the finger-popping passages in *Dancers In Love*.

2

The Duke Ellington Story *as Hollywood might do it*

by Leonard Feather

(Written after an evening at *The Gene Krupa Story*, and with memories of *The Benny Goodman Story*, *The Five Pennies* and *St. Louis Blues*.

● ● ● ● ● ● ● ●

(FADE IN: A modest living room with portrait of President McKinley on wall. Through a window we see the White House. In one corner sits a small electronic piano. A small boy, obviously not more than 1½, picks out notes. Suddenly an older man, clearly at least 18, tears open the door.)

ELLINGTON SR. *(played by Mantan Moreland):* STOP! Not another note of that immoral ragtime! Son, don't you know that's the devil's music?

BOY *(played by Sugar Chile Robinson):* Crazy, dad! When I grow up, I'll have a big band and call it Duke's Blue Devils. Now hear this. *(Resumes playing as an older woman rushes in.)*

MOTHER *(played by Moms Mabley):* What is it, son?

ELLINGTON SR.: I'll tell you what it is. Our son is bringing shame to our family name. Thirty-five years I've been a butler at the White House—I trimmed Lincoln's beard, I officiated at Andrew Johnson's impeachment, I ghosted Grover Cleveland's speeches—and now Edward here wants to reduce us all to rags! The boy *must* grow up to be a butler. He shall leave for buttling school next fall.

MOTHER: For shame! Let the child wail. Rags are the thing, so they say. Come, let's do a cakewalk. *(She attempts to dance with him, but he brushes her aside.)*

ELLINGTON SR.: Out of my house the both of you! I'm a God-fearing man, and these are Satan's cadences. Besides, he's playing all the wrong changes to *Maple Leaf Rag.*
(Enter Duke's sister, RUTH, played by Patty Duke.)

RUTH: Why, Duke, that's peachy! Play the new Jelly-Roll Morton hit, *Alexander's Ragtime Band.*

MOTHER: Duke? Who's Duke?

RUTH: Why, didn't you know? That's what all the kids at Armstrong high are calling him. They say some day he'll play for the Duke of Windsor.

DUKE (*stops playing abruptly, bows graciously*): Thank you, my dear, for making things clear. Love you madly.

RUTH: Darling, I have wonderful news. In Brooklyn they're crazy about your painting. You have an offer of a scholarship at Pratt Institute.

DUKE (*picks up paint brush in left hand, pen in right hand, idly starts sketching on canvas while scribbling on MS paper*): It's a hard decision to make. Sometimes I wonder whether my left hand knows . . .

MOTHER: Edward, whatever you do, the door is open. Your father will forgive and forget.

DUKE: Sorry, ma. Too bad, dad. I'm checking out, goodbye!

(*FADE OUT . . . FADE IN: A hot-dog stand on a New York City street corner. Ellington, now 19, played by Mercer Ellington, holds up frankfurter, shows it to* SONNY GREER, *played by Sal Mineo, and* OTTO HARDWICKE, *played by Bud Freeman.*)

ELLINGTON: This is it, gentlemen. Three weeks in New York and still they aren't ready for our music. Our last nickel went for this hot dog. Where's the slide rule? (GREER *offers him ruler.* ELLINGTON *measures off one-third of frankfurter, hands it to* GREER *and then does same for* HARDWICKE *and eats the rest.*) Say, this wiener is real George! . . . Well, I guess father was right. It's back to Washington and President McKinley's bootstraps.

GREER: Man, where you been? That cat's long gone—old man Harding's there now, Buster.

ELLINGTON: Buster Harding? Love him madly.
(*A suave, well-dressed man walks up and hands* ELLINGTON *a calling card.*)

MILLS (*played by Billy Daniels*): My name is Irving Mills. I heard you rehearsing *Star Dust* the other night and being that I publish the song, I was mighty impressed by what you did with it. Why, you played chords which they aren't even on the piano! No more Washington for you, my lad. Stick with me, and it'll be big time all the way—a Monday night at Birdland, autograph parties at Howard Johnson's, maybe even a concert at the famous La Scala opera house in Paris!

ELLINGTON, GREER, and HARDWICKE (*together*): The famous La Scala opera house in Paris?

MILLS: In Paris, France! Fellers, from now on the sky's the limit. Waiter, hot dogs all around, and don't spare the mustard!

(*FADE OUT: Calendar flips over, showing 1923-4-5-6-7-8-9. FADE IN: A gaudy night club teeming with flappers, bootleggers, Cotton club girls, sawed-off shotguns and Playmates. On a small bandstand to one side, ELLINGTON pounds furiously at piano; he is leading a 23-piece band including JOHNNY HODGES, played by Ornette Coleman; COOTIE WILLIAMS, played by Red Nichols; REX STEWART, played by Ray Anthony; BARNEY BIGARD, played by Sol Yaged; TRICKY SAM NANTON, played by Russ Morgan, and IVIE ANDERSON, played by Julie London. A pretty girl, played by Hermione Gingold, sidles up to the piano and bares her teeth.*)

ELLINGTON: Love you madly. And whose pretty little girl are *you*?

GIRL: Well, like I've been making it with the brass section, but you can just call me Pretty Little Girl. Or Girl for short. You know, when you hit those keys, something happens to my liver bile. Something bigger than both of us. You pound a dastardly ivory.

ELLINGTON: You know, you make this whole room look beautiful. You inspire me—you're such a sophisticated lady . . . say! That gives me a superb idea . . . (*turns to keyboard, fingers a few notes, hums, then stops*) . . . Eureka! Listen to this. How do you like it? I'll call it *Cotton Tail*.

GIRL: Why don't we have a drink after the show and like talk it over?

DUKE: Your wish is my command. And tomorrow night I'll bring you back so you can hear my new brass section.
(MILLS *rushes in carrying newspaper.*)

MILLS: Duke! We're ruined! Look at this headline in *Variety!* Wall Street Lays an Egg! The club is bankrupt—we're both out of a job! Well, see you around the soup kitchen. *(Exit.)*

GIRL: Come see me when you get a job, Duke. I'll be at the third apple stand on the left. *(Exit, carrying mink.) (By now the club is deserted.* ELLINGTON, *left alone in dim light, takes out picture of White House and gazes at it longingly.)*

ELLINGTON: Well, that's the way the Breakfast Ball bounces. Here I am all alone, in my solitude . . . say! That gives me an idea! *(Picks up sousaphone, starts blowing melody.)* And I have the perfect title for it—*Diminuendo and Crescendo in Blue. (As he plays, an invisible 67-piece symphony orchestra joins in. Out of the darkness emerges a sexy brunette, played by Frances Faye.)*

BRUNETTE: What's the matter, dad? Feel bad?

ELLINGTON: Well, my manager just quit, and I lost my job, and a beautiful chick walked out on me, but I still love you madly. Say, what's that you're drinking?

BRUNETTE *(through clenched teeth, sucks in breath before answering):* Passion fruit. Try some, dad. It'll make you 10 feet tall, and you'll have a ball, and that's all. (ELLINGTON *drinks. Weird music in background; double exposure photography as the whole club sways before his eyes.)*

ELLINGTON: Hey, that's keen! Who's your fruitlegger? I need a fifth.

BRUNETTE: Daddy, I got more fifths in my pad than Izzy Einstein ever impounded. Some day, when you've developed a tolerance, we'll do it up real strong—a passion fruit *cocktail.*

ELLINGTON: Not later! Not later! Now!

BRUNETTE: Okay, daddy, you asked for it! *(Leads him by hand, clutching fifth of passion fruit as they stumble out in the dark.)*

(FADE OUT . . . FADE IN: A hospital ward. ELLINGTON, *unshaven, haggard, lies in small bed cluttered with MS paper.)*

ELLINGTON: It's no good, I tell you! I can't write any more! Nurse, without passion fruit I am an empty shell! Pity me! Say, by the way, whose pretty little girl are you?

NURSE *(played by Nancy Wilson):* Now, now, we mustn't excite ourselves. *(Telephone rings offscreen. She runs to answer it and then returns.)* It's long distance—Washington.

ELLINGTON: My folks! *Now* they call me! Why didn't they remember me when I was up on top, playing the devil's music? Well, I'll talk anyway.

NURSE: I'm sorry, patients are allowed no personal calls. Besides, it was a wrong number. They were looking for *Ray* Ellington. *(MILLS enters, holding sheet of paper.)*

MILLS: Duke, where have you been? I've been looking for you ever since that night they closed up the club. I read where they framed you on that bum passion fruit rap, but then you like dropped out of sight.

ELLINGTON: I—I've been trying to make ends meet. A little sign-painting job here, a ragtime gig there whenever Willie the Lion's too busy to take one—say, what's that in your hand?

MILLS: Duke, it's your chance. Oscar Peterson was supposed to play this concert, but there was a confliction—he's booked the same night at Central Plaza, and Norman Granz thought you might be able to fill in . . .

ELLINGTON: Where? What? Who? How? Why? When?

MILLS: Oh, it's nothing really—Just a little gig at the famed La Scala opera house in Paris, on New Year's Eve.

ELLINGTON (gasps): The famed La Scala opera house in Paris?

MILLS: Of course, it's a scale date, and you have to pay the round-trip transportation for all the sidemen, plus bus fare to and from the airports. But it's a start. The road back is hard, you know. And you'll have to—ah—(glamces around nervously, whispers)—you'll have to take it easy with that passion fruit.

ELLINGTON: Aah, I've been off the stuff for years. Just give me this chance, I'll do anything. I'll even write *Mood Indigo*. Meanwhile, take these. (*Hands him huge pile of MS scattered all over bed.*) A couple of things I tossed off last night—*Don't Get Around Much Any More, Things Ain't What They Used To Be, I'm Beginning To See The Light,* and a few other fitting titles. Maybe I can get enough of an advance on these to take care of the fares?

MILLS (*looks at MS, beams*): Duke, I know you could do it! Why, these will be your biggest hits since *Rent Party Blues*. Here, be my guest. (*Pulls frankfurter out of pocket.* ELLINGTON *measures, divides it into three parts, gives a third each to Mills and nurse, and eats rest.*)

ELLINGTON (*to nurse*): Hey, little girl—what are you doing New Year's Eve?

(*FADE OUT*)

(*FADE IN: La Scala opera house.* ELLINGTON, *backstage, looks a little nervous: he is wearing swallow-tail coat back to front.*)

MILLS: Duke, stop worrying. They haven't forgotten you. Turn that coat around and go out and face them. (ELLINGTON *does so.* NORMAN GRANZ, *played by George Wein, steps to microphone.*)

GRANZ: Our next artist needs no introduction, so I won't introduce him. This, then, is Duke Ellington!

(*Audience remains coldly silent. Ellington steps to piano, goes into first chorus of* Love You Madly. *He is backed by a 973-piece orchestra with 428 strings. In center is* SAM WOODYARD, *played by Shelly Manne; near him are* HARRY CARNEY, *played by Gerry*

Mulligan; JIMMY HAMILTON, *played by Steve Allen;* JOHNNY HODGES, *played by Cannonball Adderley, and* RAY NANCE, *played by Shorty Rogers. Seated at a piano directly on top of Duke's is* BILLY STRAYHORN, *played by Bobby Troup.)*

ELLINGTON: I . . . I can't go on! They hate me madly!

MILLS: Play, Duke! You can do it! Remember, they all laughed at Whitney and his cotton gin!

(ELLINGTON plays. Orchestra swells to tremendous crescendo, stops dramatically for Ellington to play solo break. As he starts, a voice is heard from third mezzanine.)

VOICE: Hey there, passion fruit boy! Want a little taste?

2ND VOICE: There's no room for passion fruit fiends in our country! *(ELLINGTON winces but continues. Music reaches four even more tremendous crescendos, each bigger than the last. For the final chorus 265 additional musicians step onstage to lend body to the arrangement. As music ends, Duke steps forward, bows. Audience applauds thunderously.)*

AUDIENCE: Bravo! Bravissimo! Bravississimo! Love you *follement! (ELLINGTON, tears in eyes, bows again, runs off.* GIRL *is waiting in wings.)*

GIRL: Yes, daddy, I waited . . . I knew some day I'd find you here. You can still call me Pretty Little Girl if you want to.

ELLINGTON: Well, I guess I'm just a lucky so-and-so. Hey, that gives me a great idea! *(He sits at piano on the now-darkened stage and fingers keys.).* And I've got the perfect title. I think I'll call it *Tulip or Turnip.*

(They gaze longingly into each other's eyes and start to embrace. FADE OUT.)

(Note: The characters in the above screen play, despite their real names, bear no resemblance to any actual people, living or dead, and are not intended to. They are intended to resemble only the characters Hollywood would make out of them. L.G.F.)

3

Hollywood, U.S.A.

● ● ● ● ● ● ● ●

Charlie Barnet: During the early '40s I bought a home in Los Angeles and settled down. Well, let's just say I bought a home in Los Angeles.

The band was playing at the Casa Manana at the time and Kay Starr had her first job with us as vocalist. Years later, when asked what caused her occasional bouts with laryngitis, she replied: "I used to sing with Charlie Barnet's band. Fourteen cannon, a tank battalion and triple forte don't do much to improve the vocal cords."

The house was just a hop, skip and stone's throw from all points, including Birmingham General Hospital, where Desi Arnaz was stationed. Cully Richards was also doing a stint for Uncle Sam, and besides playing for the Hollywood Canteen I maintained a lesser USO at home. Lesser only in number.

They were at the house frequently, as were the boys in the band; Kurt Bloom, my band manager; George Siravo, my arranger; and a few friends and sundry acquaintances. In short, it was like 50th and Broadway.

A little animal life added to the general confusion in the form of a police dog named Lady; two monkeys named Rebop and Xavier respectively; and a giant rhesus of the chimpanzee family named Herman. I tried diligently to teach Herman the rudiments of the saxophone—unsuccessfully, I might add.

One particular night Cully, Desi and Tommy Dorsey were at the house. Desi was in the patio, babaluing a somewhat fancy lady to the accompaniment of his guitar. We forebore the first few renditions, but as time wore on our nerves did too. The repetition of the *Babalu* theme was giving us the screaming mee-mies.

We were afforded a little surcease when Desi wandered off into the night. Cully quickly brought the guitar in from the patio, solemnly handed it to Tommy, who gave it a resounding whack against the stairway bannister and then handed it to me.

By the time the guitar had made the rounds a few times it ended up a most dilapidated instrument. We cremated the remains in the fireplace and sat back to guffaw, when the thought struck us that when Desi picked up the guitar case he would notice the difference in weight.

We pondered the problem over a few more drinks, and doubtless Johnny Walker was of some help, as we found a solution:

Slightly used olives and onions, empty bottles, cigarette butts—the ashtrays needed emptying anyhow—overripe peaches, some hardly-eaten sauerkraut and several rather black bananas found their way into the case along with what was available from the garbage can.

We were all quite hilarious when Desi quite unsuspectingly carried his guitar case home.

The only fly in the ointment was that Lucy might not have found it quite as humorous as we did.

We needn't have worried.

Several weeks later the Birmingham Special Service staff held a benefit at the Los Angeles Shrine Auditorium. Desi was master of ceremonies and Tommy Dorsey, Jimmy Dorsey, Cully Richards and I were on the bill. Since Desi made no reference to what had been called Operation Garbage, we could only assume the worst. The garbage must still be in the guitar case.

At this point Desi informed us he was going to do *Babalu* and accompany himself on the guitar.

He reached for the case, but I was quicker—very quick, in fact. He kept pulling on one end and I was hanging on the other end. While we played tug o' war Tommy and Jimmy and Cully were breaking up laughing.

I finally managed to convince Desi that the audience would be much more appreciative of a bongo accompaniment than a guitar, so he gave up his end of what was now sure to be a pretty fragrant guitar case.

Desi plodded his homeward way after the benefit, the still undetected garbage in tow.

A few weeks later I was playing the Strand Theater in New York. Desi called.

"Hello, Charlie?"

"Oh, no. . . . that you, Desi?"

"Yes. That was a very funny joke. But I forgive you. But Charlie?"

"Yeah, Desi?"

"Where did you hide my guitar?"

A good question. A very good question.

:

Back in the 1940s, Joe Zucca was operating the Casa Manana, a large dining and dancing spot out in Culver City, Cal. Joe elected to book the Duke Ellington orchestra opposite our band for a battle of music.

We were all looking forward to it, though battling the Ellington orchestra is a frightening experience for any band. I had a pretty fair band as bands went by my standards, but it certainly wasn't any match for Duke's. Ensemble-wise we did all right, but as far as soloists go, we couldn't come anywhere near them of course. So we decided to use a little bit of skullduggery.

We had a meeting, and each man in my band was assigned a man in the Ellington band. The purpose was very simple: to get him drunk.

Now it seems that Joe Zucca realized there would be a melee on the bandstand while the two bands were changing, so he employed the Red Callender Trio during the changeovers.

To cut a long story short, Red Callender wound up playing about 75% of the evening. We did such a successful job of putting the Ellington band out of commission that I felt rather terrible about the whole thing. So terrible that for the last two Ellington sets, I wound up with Duke's band, playing saxophone in the chair of Otto Hardwick, who was completely out. Some of the others were in sad shape; in fact the only section that seemed to maintain any equilibrium consisted of the three gentlemen in the trombone section.

The Barnet band was doing pretty well along the same lines,

I might add. It finally wound up as one band, because by the last set there were just enough musicians available between the two bands to make one band. And the capper to the whole thing was when Wingy Manone whipped out his horn, and stepped on the bandstand beside Cat Anderson and said, "I'll take it!" And what could follow that?

Shorty Sherock: Phil Kahgan is a contractor for Paramount Studios. He talks with a sort of Russian-Jewish accent, you know, and he has a favorite thing that if anything happens in the trumpet section he'll look up from his desk, over his glasses, and he'll say, "Somebody krekked a note! Who krekked?"

One day he calls me. "Hey, Shorty, you busy this afternoon?"

"No," I said.

"Well, dress up real nice; I got a good job for you. We're going to shoot a picture and you're going to play right on the set."

I got into the car and drove to the studio and went into his office. Three of the better known trumpet players in town were sitting around there waiting.

One was Al Golden; a tall, lean, real good looking New York lawyer type.

The second was Pinky Savitt—he's kind of chubby and rotund, you know.

The third fellow was Jackie Coons, and I'm the fourth one there. Coons wasn't dressed up at all—he had dungarees on, and open-toed sandals, and sort of a faded hibiscus Hawaiian shirt. All the rest of us were kind of dressed up.

In walks Phil. "Hi, boys! The director wants to see you right away!"

We follow him downstairs, and line up against this wall, and the director comes out and he looks at us.

"Phil, baby," he says, "what's wrong? I asked for musician types!" And he points to this first guy and he says, "Not a lawyer!" And he looks at the second fellow and says "Not a butcher!" And he looks at me and he says, "Not an Irish cop!" Finally he says, "All right, kid, you're in," and he picks Jackie Coons.

Milt Raskin: One day at the MGM sound stage we found every-thing more heavily protected than usual—cops standing around guarding the studio and a general atmosphere of something drastically important about to happen.

Then Johnny Green stood up and made a big, very impressive speech for all of us musicians, ending up with something like this: "Here we have a girl who is 37 years of age, who has had her share of troubles, and who has never sung before." Dramatic pause, and then, "I'd like to introduce Miss Susan Hayward."

Of course we all applauded, and then we went into rehearsal. The songs were all pop things of the *Red Red Robin* type. At last we managed to make a take. The whole band went in to listen to the playback, but I stayed outside. I figured, after all, I'd heard it.

Jack Marshall (the guitarist) was the first to come back on the sound stage.

"Well," I said, "how was it, Jack? How did she sound to you?"

And Jack said: "Like a girl who is 37 years of age, who has had her share of troubles, and who has never sung before."

André Previn: I was conducting the orchestra for the Academy Awards, and Ella Fitzgerald was singing one of the numbers. It happened that that year I won an award, so I had to jump out of the pit and get the award; and then I ran into the wings with the Oscar in my hand, and Ella gave me a big kiss and congratu-lated me very sweetly.

Someone came up to me and said: "Mr. Previn, would you go backstage and see the press and have your picture taken."

"I don't think I'd better," I said, "I have to get back in the pit and finish the show."

And Ella said, "Sweetie, don't be ridiculous. I mean, how many times in your life does a thing like this happen? You go right ahead and have your picture taken."

And so I said, "Okay, Ella; but you're on next."

"I'm on next?" she said. "You get the hell back in the pit!"

:

The major studios, when they were still running things, used to have periodic campaigns to save money, being more strict about expenses and so forth. Around 1951 or so an edict came down saying that from now on, composers should be on the lot between 9 a.m. and 6 p.m. And if they went home at any time other than 6 p.m. they would have to call the accountant of the music department, tell them they were leaving and why they were leaving, and where they were going.

Well, of course, we screamed bloody murder; because this is not the kind of job where you put in regular hours. But there was nothing we could do about it. But by luck, within a week of the time that rule came down, I was working on a picture for which we had an impossible deadline, and I worked like a fiend.

One evening I worked until six, ran out and got a sandwich, came back to the office, and worked until four in the morning. When I finally got through and looked at my watch, I remembered the inter-office communiqué.

I found the music accountant's home number, called him, and woke the poor man out of a deep sleep. "This is André Previn," I said. "It's not 6 p.m. It's four o'clock in the morning. I want to report that I just got through and am now going home." And I hung up.

Well, the next day it paid off—they rescinded the whole thing. I was very popular around the studio for about a week.

:

The music library at MGM has saved, since about 1936, a memo that came down to the music department at that time, from Irving Thalberg.

Thalberg, as you know, was supposedly the great genius of pictures, and I'm sure he was; but music was not one of his strong leanings.

While he was running a picture, there was something in one part of the musical score that displeased him. So he said: "What is that sound?" And one of his flunkeys, who didn't know any better but felt he had to give him some kind of answer, said: "Mr. Thalberg, that's a minor chord."

And the next day, the entire MGM music department—copies

to every composer—received a memo, signed by Irving Thalberg, stating very formally that "From this date on, no score in any MGM picture is allowed to have a minor chord in it."

Peggy Lee: The wildest beat-off I ever heard was during a rehearsal, when the conductor was getting kind of bugged and wasn't thinking too clearly.

"All right, gentlemen," he said, "let's take it from the last few bars. One! Two!"

André Previn: When I did the music for *Porgy and Bess* they made a big federal secret on the Goldwyn lot about all the goings on. They didn't want anybody to know how the tracks were being recorded.

Goldwyn and I and an orchestra of about 90 were on the recording stage, and we took a break to listen to some of the music. One of the singers, Adele Addison, wanted some tea. So I said, "I feel like a walk; I'll go over to the cafe and bring back several orders of tea and doughnuts and stuff."

I am not given to dressing up when I conduct. I was wearing a sports shirt and slacks. At the cafe I borrowed one of those big rolling carts and brought back enough stuff for a large number of people. By this time Goldwyn had sent a cop over to the recording stage.

When I tried to go through, the cop said: "What do you think you're doing, trying to get in there? This is a closed set."

So I said, quite truthfully, "They sent me out for tea and doughnuts."

The cop opened the door and yelled, "There's a fellow here says he's bringing tea and doughnuts." Rouben Mamoulian, who was directing the picture at this point, said, "Sure, let him in."

For several days after this, the only way I could get into my own set was to be the tea and doughnut boy. The cop never did recognize me. Once he even came in while I was on the podium conducting. It was too nice a moment for me to spoil by saying anything. The cop looked at me benevolently and said:

"Okay now, sonny, get the hell off the podium, the conductor's liable to be here any minute!"

:

This could be called the story of the gift that bit the giver. Sammy Davis, Jr. is a generous man; he just loves to give presents. He was very happy about doing the role of Sportin' Life in *Porgy and Bess,* and before running through his big dance number *(It Ain't Necessarily So)* he wanted Mr. Goldwyn to come and see him; so they arranged to meet in the rehearsal hall.

"Before I show you the number," Sammy told him, "I have a gift for you." And he handed him a really extraordinary watch. It had an inscription on it, to Sam from Sammy, and Sammy was explaining the chronometer, and how to use the stop watch and the phases of the moon and the days of the week and everything.

"I'm very touched," said Goldwyn, "but what is this for?"

"For no reason," said Sammy, "except that I'm grateful to you and I hope you like it."

Goldwyn said, "It's wonderful; thank you very much indeed. Now, let's see the dance number."

The rehearsal pianist started, and Sammy went to work, and you know how hard he works. It was a long, elaborate number, and at the end of it Sammy did this big finish, drenched in sweat, and came to his big last pose right in front of Mr. Goldwyn.

"Well, there you have it," he said triumphantly. "How did you like it?"

Goldwyn clicked his brand new watch and looked at it.

"It's too long," he said.

:

One of the very first pictures I ever did the music for was some kind of murder mystery; the locale was New York City. It was perhaps my third picture, but the producer was a novice; it was his first.

To my complete surprise, he instructed me to use, as a theme, *Cielito Lindo.*

"You mean the Mexican song?" I said.

"That's right."

I didn't know what possible relationship it could have with the film. I thought maybe I had missed some kind of hidden symbolism. I looked at the picture again, and got more and more baffled.

I couldn't stand it any more, so I went up to his office and said: "Look, I must know. This picture is about a hospital in New York. Why, of all things, *Cielito Lindo,* which is a Mexican song?"

His answer was the only possible answer.

"Cielito Lindo," he said, "is my favorite song."

:

When I was working at MGM, many years ago, I had dealings with a man who was a very good producer but had no knowledge of music. I was writing for a picture in one scene of which, for reasons of plot, the hero and heroine had to be at a chamber music concert, and the stage had to have a piano on it. So I was told to get some famous piece of chamber music in the public domain and record it.

I thought the most popular piano quintet was the Schumann, so I took the first four chairs from the MGM orchestra and myself, and recorded the first movement. Because there were only five of us it was an unusual thing to have to record for a film of this kind; we took great pains with it and it was a successful recording.

I sent the recording to the producer's office. He called me a few hours later.

"It's beautiful," he said, "but I want you to remake it; and for Chrissake, this time use more fellers."

I tried to point out, gently, that the word "quintet" has certain inherent restrictive qualities.

"I don't care about that," he said. "It sounds lousy. Get as many men as you want!"

Boy, that was some argument. But I finally convinced him, so we didn't wind up with the world's first 99-piece quintet.

4

Getting there
is half the fun

• • • • • • • •

I may be nuts, but I still enjoy one-nighters. The fact that I never do more than one in a row may have something to do with it; nevertheless, it's fun to play with a big band, and there are still a few left.

If you're not independently wealthy, it's a good idea to save your money before becoming involved with some of these groups, because big bands are no longer big business. But people still like dance bands, and the booking agencies furnish their clients with long lists of famous bandless bandleaders. Then when the contracts are signed, the bandless bandleader who gets the nod calls his contractor, who books fifteen or sixteen men for that particular date, making sure that at least four of the men have usable cars, and away they go.

It's not really a swindle for the people who attend the dance, for sure enough, there's their famous bandleader standing in front of his band, playing the music that made him famous. What they don't know is that no matter which famous bandleader they might have selected, they would probably have gotten more or less the same band; that is, the guys who do the big band one-nighters. Of course, there are a few big bands around that work enough to keep the same men together for long periods, have their own uniforms, library, arrangers and high musical standards; but this doesn't seem to cut any ice with either the public or the booking agents. This type of band nowadays is the exception, rather than the rule.

Now, let's go on an imaginary one-nighter with Claude Clyde and his Rhythm Rascals. You're told to be at the Capitol Hotel at 9:30 Saturday morning, complete with your dark suit and your toothbrush (assuming you're relatively fastidious) and your horn. You know from experience that there is no longer any Capitol Hotel, and that the band won't actually leave until 10:15, but you show up at 9:30 where the Capitol used to be because you're a good guy.

You're the first one there. The rest of the sidemen and a few of the cars begin to straggle in at 9:50, and you're assigned to the drummer's car. He's not a great drummer, but he has this big station wagon. You are a trifle dismayed when you have to sit in the back with the jackets, library, bass, drums, and Claude's golf clubs.

You notice that the drummer is poring over maps of West Virginia, but then you remember the contractor's assurance that it's only a short hop, 150 miles or so. You're pleased to notice that the girl vocalist is also assigned to your car; this indicates that, females being what they are, there will be many rest stops.

You rearrange the vocalist's gowns so that you can once again see out the window, and the car majestically pulls out into the Eighth Avenue traffic at precisely 10:17. A wonderful feeling of camaraderie exists in the station wagon, because you're all sharing this adventure together. You tell all the jokes that you can think of to tell, and so does everyone else; however, because of the presence of the girl vocalist, this becomes a rather limited category. Then there is a short discussion of world affairs and the state of the music business. Then, as everyone runs out of conversation, the long silence sets in. This happens about the time you reach the Lincoln Tunnel, and lasts until you reach your destination, Noshe, West Virginia, eight and a half hours later.

Of course, there were some wonderful sights and smells along the way. The oil refineries, the garbage incinerators, the auto graveyards, the acres of manure. And the trip was broken up by four rest stops, two gas stops, three Howard Johnson stops, and a Dairy Queen stop. And, oh yes, one liquor stop for those with enough foresight to be concerned with the return trip.

You arrive at Noshe and have no trouble locating the center of town. You have the table d'hote dinner at the Noshe Hilton, and drive straight out to the gymnasium of the Kanawha State Teachers' College. You go to the men's locker room, find a vacant sink, and do the best you can with liquid antiseptic soap, paper towels, and your own shaving lotion. Then you just have time to get to the bandstand, look over the music, and warm up your horn. While you're doing this, you answer to the best of your ability the following questions, put to you by several eager early arrivals:

1) Is this the *real* Claude Clyde band, or just some boys he picked up in Clarksburg? You show them your 802 card.
2) How long have you been with Claude? You tell them you've been with him about 12 hours. They laugh.
3) Where do you go from here? You tell them back to New York.
4) You mean right after the job tonight? You tell them yes, it's all in the day's work. They don't believe you.
5) Does the drummer take dope? You tell them the drummer *is* a dope. They are disappointed. They go away.

Claude Clyde arrives by cab from the airport. He will check into the Noshe Hilton after the job and fly back to New York the next day. He calls out the first set of tunes, waves to the people, and gives the down beat. For the next four hours you play with Claude Clyde and his Rhythm Rascals, except for a twenty-five minute period when the past Prom Queen crowns the present Prom Queen, and eighteen brothers from Tau Upsilon (or is it Throw Upsilon?) entertain with their version of *Bloody Mary*.

It is eleven a.m. the following day when your red-rimmed eyes spot what used to be the Capitol Hotel. You know everyone in the station wagon so intimately that you hope you never see any of them again. You didn't sleep much on the way back, especially after that narrow squeak on the Jersey Turnpike, and your mouth tastes like the bottom of a birdcage, and the bottom of your birdcage doesn't feel so good either. You look in your wallet and discover that you have spent about seventeen dollars. Your pay check will probably total $32.50 after deductions, leaving you with $15.50, which is better than one dollar per hour.

As you trudge home to your well-earned rest, you start thinking about next week's gig in Providence. Shouldn't be as tough as this one was, and after all, the contractor said it was only a hundred miles or so.

5

One more for the road

Give me one for my baby, and one more for the road . . . that
long, lonesome road.

Johnny Mercer

• • • • • • • •

Shorty Sherock: Those were really rough days on the road with the Ben Pollack band. At one point, by the time we got to Marshall City, Iowa, it was so cold that my feet were frozen. The roads were blocked and we found ourselves stuck in a hotel room, me with my frozen feet and all, for a solid week. When we tried to get out of town, the police would stop us at the city limits. And Pollack himself was back in Chicago, but he'd wire the band $100 a day.

This new game had just come out—Monopoly. We bought a board, and that was how we passed the time; just sitting in our hotel rooms, hour after hour, nothing but wine and monopoly and monotony.

There's no end to that story, except that according to the monopoly figures I think another trumpet player in the band wound up owing me $2,560,000. Maybe he could pay it today, come to think of it. It was Harry James.

:

Irving Fazola, the great clarinetist in the Pollack band—he died in 1949—was all music. One time we were traveling from Indianapolis to Evansville in the rain, and the going got worse and worse, until finally visibility was practically nil, and our car skidded into a ditch and turned over.

Fazola was thrown clear, but when I looked over at him I saw he had a nasty gash on the head and was bleeding badly.

"Everything all right, Faz?"

Faz pulled his precious clarinet out of the shattered case and held it up. "I think so," he said, wiping the blood off his forehead, "but I won't be sure until I've tried it out with a new reed." And he put the horn together and started blowing scales.

Gus Bivona: There was the time Charlie Barnet's band was up in Frisco and it was so hot, the guys wanted to go swimming. So they filled all the cracks in the door of one of the hotel rooms with rags and towels, and then they turned the bathtub on and let it overflow. After they got about a foot-and-a-half or two feet of water on the floor, they started diving in from the bureaus and couches.

Finally the ceiling below them leaked through and the hotel people checked. The manager called Barnet up there, and Barnet took one look and said, "Why, you miserable unprintables! The least you could have done was invite me."

Charlie Barnet: We were playing up in Canada when the war broke out and there was a good deal of confusion. These two guys and myself got to fooling around in Toronto and we missed the train that was supposed to take us to our next date in Youngstown, Ohio.

So we hired a taxi to take us to Buffalo and catch the train. We got about halfway down the line when this other guy suddenly remembered he left his trumpet at the hotel.

By the time we got back to Buffalo we had missed the train again. We would have made it, only at the border they wouldn't believe we were Americans. Well, we had to hire a plane to take us to Cleveland from Buffalo, and in Cleveland we grabbed another taxi to Youngstown. We got there just when the last set was over, and it cost me more than I made in a month.

That isn't all. The next night we had a date in Akron. I decided not to get mixed up with these two guys again, but I got into a little trouble on my own, and missed the train for Akron.

I called the airport and said I wanted to charter a plane, in my own name. The guy at the airport told me I couldn't be Charlie Barnet because Charlie Barnet just chartered a plane for Akron. Of course, it was the two boys who got into trouble in Toronto, and one of them passed himself off as me in order to charter the plane.

Well, I told them to hold the plane until I got to the airport, and dashed madly out there. There were my two boys, standing around looking sheepish. I yelled plenty when I discovered they

71

had chartered a 3-passenger plane and there were five of us, counting the pilot.

We finally all got into the plane, and after about ten minutes we were in a snowstorm, and before we could shake it we were in Wheeling, which is further from Akron than Youngstown is.

That's about all, except that the pilot wouldn't take us up again in the storm, so we had to get a cab for Akron from Wheeling, and we were late for the date again.

:

Curry Wilson was my friend and property man for about fifteen years. Everybody just called him Wilson, and we even had a tune in the books dedicated to him: *Wilson, That's All.*

Wilson was a very important man on the bus; he had one of those big Coca-Cola boxes filled up with ice, and he'd make what we called the "Wilson Bomber." He'd pour out half the coke and fill the bottle up with whiskey. He sold beer and cokes too.

One day Wilson announced that he had to raise the prices on everything except the Bomber. There were a lot of complaints about it, but Wilson explained about the rising costs: "It costs money for ice, you know," he said.

One day during the same cold winter we looked out the back of the bus during a rest stop, and there was Wilson diligently shoveling up snow and ice for his box! And that was how we brought the prices down again.

Georgie Auld: Bunny Berigan—now that was about the wildest band that was ever organized—*un*organized. I was in Bunny's sax section when I was eighteen.

Once Bunny fell down and broke his ankle. He had his foot put in a cast and had a sock pulled over the toe and just as it would be ready for the cast to come off he'd fall and break it all over again.

Things were so rough that the chick with the band reached the point where she just couldn't take it any more. Jane Dover, that was her name. One night there was only one seat left on the bus, and that was next to her. Johnny Napton, the trumpet player, wanted to take it, and she wouldn't let him. So he started cursing her out.

She started to run out of the bus. "I can't take this any more!" she told Bunny. "All this rotten language, this foul-mouthed talk, I'm through!"

Bunny, who has had one more for the road and then some, gets back on the bus with her and all the guys are seated in their chairs. He grabs the post beside the driver, starts banging on it with his cane and just about breaks the cane in half. He's furious.

"I've had it! All this language, and the girl singer wants to quit the band, and you're hanging me up in the middle of a stack of one-nighters without a girl singer! Now I want you to get one thing straight! (The girl is sitting there while he's saying all this.) The first ——— ———— that curses on this bus is automatically through!"

Everybody on the bus starts to laugh, so he catches himself and says, "Well, I didn't mean to put it that way, but I'm serious! I don't want to hear another foul word out of any of you as long as Jane is sitting in this bus!"

Well, we go about 250 miles, and not a sound out of anyone. The cats were even lighting their cigarets real quiet because we knew Bunny was flipping.

Along about daybreak, Joe Bushkin, our pianist, is in the back of the bus, and just as everybody's starting to open their squinty eyes Bushkin runs down the bus, and he stops by the driver and turns around facing everybody, including Bunny, and yells:

"I can't stand it any longer! ——! ——! ——— ———!" and every other word he can think of.

That was without doubt the most frantic bunch of kids that were ever together.

Milt Raskin: I was playing piano with Gene Krupa's band, and there was this guy who was not only a bad trumpet player but a drunk, and addicted to foul language, too.

We were on the bus and it must have been about five in the morning. My ex-wife and I were sitting in back of this trumpet player, and Anita O'Day, Krupa's vocalist, was sitting in front of him. This cat would wake up out of a stupor and start to bother Anita. And she'd wake up and look back and say "Let me alone," but he'd just keep bothering her.

So she stood up and walked back to his seat, pulled him up and out into the aisle, planted her feet squarely and just belted him and knocked him out cold. Then she went back to her seat, curled up comfortably and went back to sleep.

Carlos Gastel: In the early days of my association with Nat Cole as his manager, when the King Cole Trio was just beginning to make some noise, we went out and did a series of one-nighters with Benny Carter's band, Savannah Churchill and Timmie Rogers. We got to Chicago, the city where Nat was raised. We played a new theater between the loop and the South Side.

Opening day the place was jam-packed. The trio closed the show, and after that opener that he always used to use, *The Man With The Little White Keys,* Nat went into *Gee, Baby, Ain't I Good To You.* You know how the song goes. A very romantic lyric, and the house was just so quiet you could hear a pin drop. Nat got to the part where he sings, "I bought you a fur coat for Christmas and a diamond ring . . ."

And some guy stood up in the balcony and shouted, "You ain't bought ——, man!"

Another guy stood up and said, "Yeah, I know you're right—I went to school with this cat!" And in a matter of moments the whole place was in a complete uproar.

What the hell are you going to say? There was only one thing to do. We closed the curtain.

I doubt very much that Nat would get that kind of interruption today.

Bob Fitzpatrick: I was playing trombone with Stan Kenton back in the days when Stan was driving his own car between dates. We had a two-day job at Virginia Military Institute in Lexington, Virginia.

The band bus arrived in plenty of time on the first day and we all checked in; but nobody could find Stan.

It got to be pretty tense; five minutes before the job was to start he still wasn't there. But just as we were about to hit, Stan and his wife Ann Richards, who was singing with the band, came roaring in.

One of those simple mistakes that happen all the time on one-nighter tours: Stan had driven to Lexington, Kentucky—a mere 450 miles away.

When he discovered his mistake he had chartered a plane to fly from one Lexington to the other; then he had the pilot stand by for four hours while we were playing. After that he flew Stan right back to Lexington #1 to pick up his car and drive back to Lexington #2 just in time for the afternoon concert.

:

I guess there are times in every band's career when the constant state of fatigue becomes too much.

At the Royal Albert Hall in London in 1956, Stan swung into the ad lib piano solo of the band's third selection, *Collaboration*. As he finished, I walked over to the microphone, ready to follow with my trombone solo. Then my mind went blank. All I could remember was which band I was with.

I walked over to the piano and said to Stan, "What the hell are we playing?"

"You know something?" said Stan. "I've forgotten too, Fitz." Then he went over to the mike and tried to explain our goof to 7000 people and why it happened.

Herb Ellis: We were playing with Jimmy Dorsey in New York at the old 400 Club. A couple of the guys backstage found a mouse which they captured alive with the bright idea of putting it in Jimmy's horn, his alto sax, and they figured he'd go on stage and pick up his horn and the mouse would jump out and it would be a big laugh.

Jimmy plays the first tune but he only plays clarinet so nothing happens. For the second tune he picks up his saxophone and everybody in the band is waiting to see the mouse jump out but the mouse has gone the other way—up the horn. So Jimmy blows and nothing happens.

He looks in the bell and looks at the mouthpiece. Finally, the guy that put the mouse in says, "Here, let me see if I can figure out what's wrong." He fools around and then, at last, out jumps the mouse; it runs right smack into the middle of the dance floor and sits there.

Well, there was a complete riot—women screamed and ran back to their tables—two waiters came out with brooms and managed to capture it. After that we always kidded Jimmy about being the only bandleader in town who had a horn with a mousepiece.

Shorty Sherock: We were on tour with Tommy Dorsey, and there was Chuck Peterson and Jimmy Blake and the pianist was Joe Bushkin.

We got off the bus in high spirits. We were all kidding around and decided to go up to somebody's room, and we all had a taste, and everyone was rolling around the room, generally acting very crazy.

So Joe Bushkin stuck his head out the window and somebody was grabbing a hold of his legs and he was leaning out the window screaming, "Help! Help!"

Well, people down on the street were all going to work, it was around eight in the morning, and they started pointing up toward the window; and the first thing we knew the fire department was there with the net and the whole thing, and people are running up and down the halls, and running in the room, and the hotel manager sent a wire to Petrillo, to have us all thrown out of the union.

Finally everything calmed down, and the house detectives were convinced we were all finally asleep, and we were kind of seeing that the coast was clear, so we got up to this one door along the hall that was closed. And we thought somebody we knew was probably in there, because we had most of the rooms along this hall.

So we open the door, and who is lying on top of the bed, after just taking a shower, and with no clothes on, but Tommy's vocalist, Connie Haines. And she begins to scream, and the whole thing starts all over again!

:

We were doing the Kate Smith television show, with Jimmy Dorsey; and for the pièce de résistance at the end they say, "And now, here is the mother of Jimmy Dorsey!"

So Kate Smith starts to chat with her on the air: "How are you in the big city? Don't you feel kinda lost?"

And Mom with that Irish brogue of hers—she was in her seventies then I guess; she just recently celebrated her 88th birthday—Mom says: "Oh, no everything's fine; I have a companion, a lady's maid—she's not with me today, though."

"Where is she?" says Kate Smith.

"She's in the hospital. Grace is an old maid, and she's in the hospital having something taken out. If you ask me," she says, "she should have something put in."

:

Mom loved Jimmy and loved to travel in the band bus with us. They'd buy her one of these big bags of peanuts in the burlap sack, and she liked to sit in the front seat right behind the driver. And she'd sit there eating the peanuts, mile after mile.

This one night, we'd just left New York and were on our way to Toledo, Ohio. Well, everybody was feeling pretty good before they got on the bus (we used to call the bus the "Flying Bladder"), and everybody would sit there with their cans of beer. Well, this could go on just so long, and then Nature would have to take over.

There was one trombonist whose capacity was just limitless. He was finally halfway off to sleep, in the seat right behind Mom Dorsey.

There was another guy in the band who was very unpopular. He was always getting into arguments and voicing his opinions. So this fellow in back of Mom Dorsey had to go, and he was half asleep, and he got up out of the seat and looked in the front two seats—the bus is dark except for a little light above the driver's head.

He stumbled around in the dark until he got to this one guy we were not very fond of. Well, to cut a long story short, when this guy woke up he was not as dry as he had been when he'd gone to sleep. And Mom Dorsey turned around and calmly expressed what

I guess was the opinion of all of us, but we hardly expected to hear it from her.

"Well," she said, "and sure it couldn't have happened to a nicer boy!"

Herb Jeffries: Juan Tizol was always the practical joker in the Duke Ellington band. We were at a theater in Detroit and he had just bought some sort of powder that could be put in shoes; once it melted it had a vile odor.

A new trumpet player, Wallace Jones, a quiet, keep-to-himself sort of fellow, had joined the band; and during one of the rest periods between the four or five shows a day we were doing, Tizol put this crystally powder in Wallace's shoes.

Everyone got up on the bandstand; and you know those guys, when they got a real swinging number going, could get pretty hot; and Ellington used to light the stage very dramatically. He was a master at lights and illusion.

Suddenly this awful odor starts coming from Wallace. All the guys are staring at him and they start to move away; Tizol, who is in the trombone section below him, is breaking up. And Ellington was having a conniption. He was always a great stickler for decorum and for everything to go off right, and he sees all his guys separating and breaking up and finally moving off the stage in the middle of the number, leaving poor Wallace just sitting there alone, mystified.

Ellington didn't find out who had done it until several days later, when for some reason he shook hands with Tizol. The show began a few minutes later and when Ellington started to play, he almost went out of his mind. Tizol had managed to get itching powder all over his hands.

Jack Tracy: There is the tale about the three trumpet players who once auditioned for Woody Herman. The two who arrived first came neatly dressed in button-down shirts and tweed jackets, flannel slacks, discreetly polished shoes, and black knit ties. They opened red-velvet-lined cases to disclose gleaming, ornately-engraved horns rubbed to a high finish.

One at a time they took over the third trumpet chair and sat in with the section. They played all right, but nothing really happened.

Then a mangy, seedy cat walked in. The soles were out of his shoes, a dirty T-shirt and faded sweater lapped out over his greasy GI suntans, and a straggly, two-day growth of pale-red beard popped out on his sallow face. A torn, brown-paper bag held a tarnished silver cornet that looked like a reject from John Philip Sousa's "B" team.

But then he sat down in that same seat, sneaked one quick look at the music, calmly waited for the down beat, confidently put the horn to his lips . . . and played the worst.

Terry Gibbs: One time Flip Phillips and Bill Harris bought a rubber, life-size mannequin and dressed it up in some groovy clothes. It looked very real.

They took it up to their hotel room, which was on the sixth floor, opened up the window, and started screaming and yelling. Pretty soon a whole bunch of people were looking up at them, and that's when they pushed the mannequin out. When it hit the sidewalk, it must have bounced back up about 50 feet, and when it came down again, they had Nat Wexler, the bandboy, waiting. He caught it in his arms on the first bounce and calmly walked back into the hotel with it.

I guess some of those people are still trying to figure out what happened.

:

Serge Chaloff, the baritone saxophonist who was a poll winner all through the early be-bop years, had a lot of hobbies, some of them unusual for a jazz musician. At one time he was experimenting with an air pistol. When the band reached Akron for a one-nighter, Serge accidentally shot a hole through the door of his hotel room.

"You'll have to pay for it," the manager informed him. "This will cost you $24."

"If I pay for it," said Chaloff, "I'll keep it." He handed over the $24, went back to his room, unhinged the door, and the two of us walked out of the hotel, lugging it along, headed for the band bus and a date in Dayton.

Herb Jeffries: I was singing at a club in Las Vegas. One night after work I borrowed Mickey Rooney's plane and flew it to Los Angeles.

The next day I was so tired that instead of flying it back myself I decided to take another pilot with me, and later put him on a commercial plane and send him back to L.A. I was really worn out, so I went to sleep on the plane.

When I woke up it was dark.

My God, I thought, where are we? We should have been in Vegas before sundown! The pilot says, "I think Las Vegas is right over that next range." I looked at the altimeter: 7000 feet.

"Man," I said, "get this thing up in the air—you're lost!"

He said he wasn't, and gave me the signal, and there it was, *bleep bleep bleep;* as long as you are on a beam you hear that. Well, we were on a beam but it wasn't any Las Vegas beam.

I got on the radio and tried to pick up a reading. Then I looked at the fuel gauge and saw we had just a half hour of gas left. In pitch black dark night, flying over the Sierra Mountains, man!

"I've got news for you, Dad," I said. "In a half hour we have to have this thing on the ground or she's gonna stop flying."

"There's a glow over there," he said, "let's head for that; I think it's a city." We flew to this glow on the horizon, and it was a dam, they were doing night-time construction work on it.

"There it is! Boulder Dam!" he says.

"No, I was at Boulder Dam yesterday and there's no construction work being done on it. Let me see if I can get a tower around here."

What we had seen was the Davis Dam right out of Needles, California. I couldn't even get a weather signal, so I finally started signaling May Day.

My May Day signal was finally picked up by a ham operator. I don't know to this day who he was, but I wish I could thank him for saving our lives. He quickly lined up a lot of cars and had them form a pattern with their headlights to guide us.

Before long we were entirely out of gas. We sheared off the tops of some trees while we tried to head toward the lights, and finally crashed. I woke up in the Santa Fé Railroad Hospital. The pilot wasn't badly injured, but I had bruises all over my body, and cuts all over my face; I was a mess. And Needles is like the blast furnace of the world—around 120 degrees in the shade by noon the next day.

Eventually my musical director, Dick Hazard, came up and moved me to another hospital in Las Vegas. But the payoff was the Vegas club owner's reaction when I called him from Needles right after the accident. Here I was, feeling and looking like a piece of chopped liver, and after I told him what happened, you'll never guess what he said:

"Look, Needles isn't that far away. Can you try to make the second show tonight?"

Whitey Mitchell: Pete Rugolo, a classic example of the theory that Nice Guys Finish Last, organized a twenty-one piece band from New York about ten years ago. The band was supposed to play Birdland, do an album, and go on tour with a package variety show modestly called *The Greatest Show of '54*. We played Birdland, did the album, and then started on the tour. At this juncture, several prominent players suddenly became ill and begged off the tour. Pete was too much the gentleman to engage in petty bickering, so he let them out of their contracts, hired last minute replacements, and away we went. Herbie Mann was a member of this band, and was perhaps the only member who had never been west of the Hudson River, so naturally, they made him road manager. Our first stop, an auditorium in Norfolk, Virginia, was smashed to pieces the night before we were to get there by Hurricane Hazel, and from that point on, the tour went steadily downhill.

That year was the year that all the promoters suddenly decided that Norman Granz really had something, with his *Jazz At The Philharmonic,* and so there were at least eight large shows making the circuit simultaneously, and they all lost money. That was also the year that Rock 'n' Roll first made a dent on the public consciousness, and everywhere we went, the high spot of the show was not the band, was not George Kirby, was not Peggy Lee, was not Billy Eckstine. It was a ragtail group of urchins called The Drifters, whose entire music library consisted of three guitar parts scratched on schoolbook composition paper with ball point pen.

As we limped along from one half-filled house to another, the applause for the Drifters ringing in our ears, we sensed disaster, and the experienced sidemen among us (I regret to say I was not one of them) began drawing heavily against their salaries. This technique is an excellent one, which I now heartily endorse but, as it turned out, was not necessary on this particular tour. Peggy Lee and Billy Eckstine declined to press for their guarantees when the tour was canceled, so that the rest of the troupe and the band could be paid, but there aren't many performers like those two.

To make a long story short too late: One night, as our bus hurtled through the gloom toward our next half-filled auditorium, we spied a nice looking Italian restaurant along the road and persuaded Pete and the bus driver to stop. The size of our group temporarily panicked the restaurant people, but they came through with flying colors, and the food was excellent. As we were finishing up the espresso and the spumoni, one member of the band jumped up (it may well have been one of those experienced sidemen I was telling you about) and announced, "Pete's gonna pay the check!" we all began cheering, whistling, and stomping, and singing loud choruses of *For He's A Jolly Good Fellow,* and Pete, when the blood came back to his face, began poking through his wallet. With the help of Herbie Mann and some of the company funds, he indeed *did* pay the check, and we led him dazedly back to the bus.

I sometimes wonder if it was at that exact moment that Pete decided to return to the comfort of the west coast studios.

Shelly Manne: When Stan Kenton had the real big band, the *Innovations* orchestra that made the tour in 1950, there were so many men that we had to be divided up into two busloads. One was what we called the "balling bus"—you know, everybody living it up. I was on the other bus.

One day a musician from the balling bus visited us for a couple of minutes. He looked around in obvious surprise, then went back and made a report to the fellows in the other bus.

"Do you know what they're doing in there?" he said. "They're *reading!*"

Whitey Mitchell: Lester Young called up his drummer one day to book him for a concert in Pittsburgh. The drummer reluctantly accepted the job for $25. and then was horrified to learn that he would have to furnish his own transportation. He complained that transportation alone would run more than $25. "Listen, baby," said Lester, "you've gotta learn to save your money to make them out of town gigs."

Bob Bain: I was on tour with a band that included Johnny Fresco, who played tenor saxophone, and doubled on cello.

We were somewhere in New Jersey when Johnny received a good offer to join the American Broadcasting Company staff in Hollywood. So he turned in his notice. When he left he took his tenor along, but asked the manager to ship the cello back to him.

Well, the manager was pretty bugged at Johnny's leaving the band, but he didn't refuse to cooperate. He sent the cello back to Johnny all right. He sent it by freight, via the Panama Canal. I think it reached Johnny about eight months later.

Herb Ellis: When we landed in Tokyo with *Jazz At The Philharmonic,* there were thousands of people at the airport. There was a real red carpet out, people brought wreaths of flowers, they had a ticker tape parade—the works.

Oscar Peterson had bought all new clothes for the trip, and when we got to the theater there he was in a beautiful new suit. We went out onstage and started right out cookin'.

Now, you know, those people are small, so I guess they make the piano stools smaller. All of a sudden I'm playing and I don't hear any piano. I hadn't been playing guitar with Oscar too long, so I didn't even look over—I thought he was just laying out. But finally I turned around and there's no Oscar, just a piano there. I

83

looked at Ray Brown and said, "Where is he?" Then I saw him, flat on his back, looking up at the ceiling.

The stool had broken, and he just lay there, saying to himself, "Oscar Peterson, here you are in your new suit in Tokyo and you are flat on your back!"

Well, Norman Granz was screaming, and they finally brought Oscar another stool, and he sat down again and started to play. Soon we hear c-r-r-rash! again, and now Oscar's just hovering over the piano, trying to play it standing up.

That was Oscar's big debut in Tokyo.

:

Ray Brown is a very friendly guy and quite a talker, in addition to being about the best bass player you'll ever hear. During our Tokyo stand, he played behind Ella Fitzgerald on her set, but Oscar Peterson didn't.

Ella has a very sensitive ear—she can hear every sound within a block. So just before she went on, Oscar and Norman Granz got Ray's attention and one of them untuned his bass by loosening up the strings a little. They kept him talking until Ray had to rush onstand at the beginning of Ella's set. He played the first two bars, and it's like he was playing on rubber bands. Ray glared offstage at Oscar and yelled, "I won't forget this!"

On the next show, we came to the portion where everybody plays a ballad. Just before Oscar was due, I saw Ray leaning over the piano. Then, out came Oscar from one side, Bill Harris from the other, both very dignified. Oscar sat down, started to play, and it's nothing but b-r-r, b-r-r, b-r-r, no matter what chord he tried.

He looked in at the strings, saw a lot of little steel balls bouncing all over them, and immediately guessed what had happened. So he started grabbing them and throwing them at Ray's bass, and Bill Harris got into the act and started playing the trombone with his foot like George Brunis, and the whole joint was up for grabs.

I'm still not sure what they really thought about us in Japan.

The next year we were in Italy, and Granz was very proud the way we were breaking it up. So he talked Oscar into singing a tune during the trio's set.

Now, in those theaters over there they serve all kinds of drinks backstage, so Bill Harris got very industrious, took a tray, and gathered up a whole gang of glasses and cups and dishes, piled them up good and high, and perched the whole thing on top of a ladder.

I guess you know what happened. Norman's at the back of the theater, Oscar's a little nervous about singing, anyway, and just as he sings, "The evening breeze, caressed the trees . . ." comes this horrible crash from backstage. Bill had tipped the ladder over, and it was one of those things that lasted forever . . . bang! splang! crash! crash! rattle, rattle! tinkle . . . . CRASH!

Well, Norman jumps this high and comes screaming down the aisle and runs backstage. The first thing he sees is Bill Harris sauntering out of the dressing room, very nonchalant, big cigar in his mouth, saying, "Dammit, what's going on here?! What's all this noise about?"

Norman was so mad that we didn't dare tell him for a year.

Jack Tracy: This is one of those stories that everybody agrees *could* have happened, whether it did or not.

When Art Blakey and his Jazz Messengers first were organized, Art spent a good deal of his time, both on and offstand, preaching about the future of jazz, fervently telling all within earshot of its worth and validity.

Once, while the group was in its station wagon on one of those interminable trips between dates, the Messengers passed through a small town and, noticing a good-sized crowd gathered in the middle of a block, stopped to take a look and stretch their legs.

As they approached they saw it was a burial. Curious, they pushed closer to the cluster of people.

Intoned the minister, "Does anyone have anything to say about the deceased?"

Silence.

He repeated the statement.

More silence.

At which point Art stepped forward and said huskily, "If there is nothing to say about the deceased, I hope no one minds if I say a few words about jazz."

:

Over the years, among the most exciting of bands has been that of Lionel Hampton, with an evening's workout usually capped by a frenzied version of *Flying Home*.

During the '40s, Hamp played a one-nighter at an Army Air Force base and the band, as usual, was set up on risers. Except in this case, the top riser was a narrow one, and Hamp had his drummer up there.

During a tune late in the evening, the drummer got careless and toppled backwards to the floor. As he lay there stunned and inert, Hamp rushed over to him and cried solicitously, "Man, you think you'll be able to make *Flying Home*?"

6

Hi-Fi fable I:
The class treatment

• • • • • • • •

All the cats in the band felt the same way about Arnie Wilson. "I've never worked for anyone quite like Arnie," they used to say.

I used to say it, too. It wasn't a question of salaries; in fact, most of the guys gave Arnie a big break on the loot when he told them how rough things were. We worked for the lowest pay in any name band. In return, Arnie said the nicest things about us any leader ever said.

"That dumb, no-talent Hal O'Toole may pay more bread, but he'll never get a trombone section to sound like you make ours sound," he'd tell me.

Hal O'Toole was Arnie's big rival and the cat he hated most on earth. There was nothing he wanted more than to have a band as important and famous as O'Toole's.

"One of these days we'll play a joint where the piano is worthy of my piano player," he'd tell Larry Gray, when Larry had to play on a box with 44 broken keys. And Larry would grin and thank him.

Another thing, Arnie would ride along in the bus with us instead of hopping a plane like some leaders do. "I don't dig being undemocratic," he used to say. As for the race bit—well, he said, "If ever I have to choose between keeping Jimmy and getting southern bookings, I don't have to tell you what I'll do." And he'd put his arm around Jimmy Asher and we'd all feel good and warm and American.

Of course, this was kind of theoretical, because nobody ever tried to book us in the south. Not until this one time, when we had a date in a town not far from Atlanta. It was the only way to fill in a booking gap after a rough run of luck. Arnie was worried. He cursed everyone from Allied Booking to Governor Faubus.

"Morally and musically, we can't go without Jimmy—and yet

we can't go with him," he said. "I can't hurt Jimmy's feelings by not using him, but I can't cause him the embarrassment he'd suffer if I took him along."

Then came his brainstorm, "By God, I've got it!" he said suddenly. "I know how we can get these southern cats to accept Jimmy without even knowing it!"

The idea he had was tricky, but with Arnie everything involving hi-fi was a cinch. He was the kind of engineering and tape recording bug that carries around ten grand worth of equipment on every gig.

So, as long as Jimmy was the most valuable soloist in the band, and as long as half the arrangements were built around Jimmy's trumpet work and nobody could replace him, said Arnie, why not pre-record all his solos and feed them through the p.a. system while a dummy ofay musician went through the motions?

Pretty weird scheme, everybody agreed—but one thing was true: this way, the pure white citizens of Georgia would be applauding the work of a great Negro soloist in an invisibly integrated band!

I heard later that Arnie offered Jimmy his regular pay for the night, even though he didn't have to work; *plus* a $25 bonus. We were to meet him the following night on the gig in Cincinnati. "This was the class treatment and I could see at once he really dug it," Arnie said. "He promised he wouldn't forget the way I'd handled this problem."

Anyhow, a couple days before the Georgia gig we had a whole day in Detroit and Arnie set up all the equipment in his hotel room. He and Jimmy went through every important piece in the book that featured Jimmy, and with the help of a metronome they cut every solo so it would fit in at the exact time when the band played it on the job.

It was a long, rough ordeal for Jimmy, he told me when I asked him about it many months later. He didn't get paid extra for this, but Arnie was very thoughtful, sending out for a jug every once in a while and getting room service to supply meals—the whole bit. When you consider that he had Jimmy working on the tapes for fifteen solid hours, that must have run into quite a taste.

So the band played the date in Georgia. The hall was one of

those big cow-palace joints and the promoter was a red-faced, bald-headed cat named Sam Reston who was a big-shot local businessman. The way we heard it, he was a jazz fan and liked to book bands occasionally into this hall, which he owned.

Arnie's band boy, Al Cellini, who was a hi-fi bug, too, worked the tape machine offstage and wired things up so it would sound like every trumpet solo was really being played by Stan Nordstrom, the blond-haired cat Arnie had hired to sub for Jimmy that night.

It was no cinch to turn the machine on and off at exactly the right second. Once or twice Al goofed and the entire trumpet chorus would be two beats late. But Arnie said: "Listen, man, these Georgia squares don't know the difference. Maybe we could even have gotten away with not using Jimmy tonight, even on tape."

"So why don't we try the next set without him?" I suggested.

And that's what we did. But when it came time for a trumpet solo, Nordstrom goofed so bad that Arnie changed his mind again. After all, when you go for a high D and come out with C-sharp and then try for two whole measures to bring it up to correct pitch, as this cat did on *Sweet Lorraine,* even a Georgia square is liable to notice something is wrong. Nordstrom not only was no Jimmy Asher; he wasn't even no Henry Busse.

So the next set we went back to the original routine of piping in Jimmy. And you can guess what happened. Here we go into the arrangement of *Embraceable* and when it comes time for Jimmy's beautiful ballad solo in E-flat, Al flips on the recorder and out comes Jimmy—blowing *Sweet Lorraine* in G. Nobody had thought to run the tape forward to skip the tunes from the set before. Panicsville, U.S.A.

Luckily that was the last set of the night. Toward the end I saw Sam Reston's assistant (Reston was out sick and missed the gig) shouting something at Arnie, but nobody seemed to get it because the band was blowing its brass off. After the gig we were all too beat to talk things over, and the next day in the bus Arnie was strangely quiet, like something was on his mind.

Well, we hit the hotel in Cincinnati and Arnie ran right into Jimmy in the lobby.

"Man, did we miss you last night!" he said. "I wouldn't take a gig without you again for any money."

"Arnie," said Jimmy quietly, "I'm afraid you're going to have to."

"Have to what? What do you mean?" Arnie was a little pale.

"Well, you see, I took advantage of the night off to sit in with Hal O'Toole's band on a gig in Dayton, and Hal offered me a very good deal. Hundred a week more than you pay me, plus a contract with escalator clauses and a written promise to take me along on any job they play—anywhere!"

Luckily I had a bottle of pretty good bourbon in my pocket. I don't think anything but that, or smelling salts, would have saved Arnie at that moment . . .

Things were pretty tense on the job that night. Arnie excused Jimmy from finishing out his notice. Fact is, I don't think he ever wanted to face Jimmy again.

But that was only the half of it.

Next day we hit Chicago, and almost as soon as the bus pulled up outside the hotel, there was Freddy Samuelson from the Allied Booking office.

"Arnie," he said, "did you read the contract on that Georgia date?"

"Read it? Well, I signed it—just like I sign dozens of contracts every time I'm in the office. What do you mean?"

"The contract had a specific clause added, guaranteeing that Jimmy Asher would be present that night. Sam Reston happens to be one of the greatest living Asher fans and he's built up a tremendous local following for the kid. He says you claimed Asher was sick, but he has proof he was working that night. He's filing charges against you with the Union and frankly, Arnie, this is one case you can't win."

"But . . . but . . ." Arnie's face resembled a sheet of parchment out of the Metropolitan Museum. "We didn't take him along because of the segregation setup. Like, I thought Reston wouldn't want him. . . . I mean . . ." His voice trailed off.

"Reston is the most powerful man in that entire county. He had everything fixed with the police, not only to let Jimmy play, but to put him up in the best white hotel in town."

This time neither bourbon nor smelling salts would have helped. To cut a long story short, Arnie himself didn't make the gig that night. Nervous strain, the doctors called it.

Well, like I said, I never worked for anyone quite like Arnie Wilson. And the way things worked out, if I never have to again, like, it ain't going to bother me. You see, Jimmy helped to get me a much better job at twice the money. I'll be frank with you. Working for Hal O'Toole is one job I dig the most.

7

You can't tell the difference when the sun goes down

I'd love to have a little boy some day with red hair, green eyes and a black face—who plays piano like Ahmad Jamal.

Miles Davis

• • • • • • • •

André Previn: About 1950 I was playing at a jazz concert in Baltimore, and at the time it so happened that both the drummer and the bass player with me were Negroes. After I was through with my set I went next door to a diner.

I was at the counter having coffee and waiting for the show to end so we could leave for the next town and two men came in and sat down and kept looking at me.

Finally they asked whether I was not the man they had just heard play next door; I said yes. They paid me some very nice compliments; and then they said, "We know that you also play classical music, and are very busy in Hollywood, and what we don't understand is, and the advice we would like to give you is, a man of your obvious capabilities, why the hell don't you play with people of your own kind?"

So I said, "Well, to tell you the truth, I wanted to, but I couldn't find two other Jews that swing."

:

About five years ago Shelly Manne's group and my trio did a series of concerts up and down the coast. In Portland we played a very successful concert.

A very collegiate young man came up afterwards, with the saddle shoes, and said that his fraternity had taken over the country club and if we wanted to come there would be food and drink and some people to meet. This being not exactly the most stimulating town in the world in the evening, we said fine.

So we all met in front of the country club, and it was the perfect illustration of "Gentleman's Agreement," nothing but blond crew cut young chaps in saddle shoes and girls in white tulle dresses, going by in droves, and we were kind of worn out from the concert and looked it. So we debated a little bit about it. It was down a flight of stairs, in a kind of sous-étage.

Suddenly Shelly realized that his band and my trio consisted

94

entirely of Jewish boys, with the exception of Joe Gordon, Shelly's trumpet player, who is Negro.

He turned to Joe Gordon and said, "Joe, you go down first; if they let you in we're cool."

Joe topped it. He said, "Don't worry about a thing; I'll send out sandwiches!"

•

One night George Shearing dropped his two Negro sidemen off at their hotel. As he was headed back to his own home the taxi driver turned to him and said, "Why do you have colored musicians in your group?"

Meekly George inquired: "What color are they?"

George Shearing: Ever since I first came to this country I have always had a mixed group, and I'm sure I had the first colored manager in the business for a white group.

His name happens to be John Levy, and there's a very funny story that really proves the narrowness of people, and the significance, or lack thereof, of the visual aspect of things.

We were in St. Louis and there was a right hand man of a disc jockey there—one of the guys who makes out the program, pulls out the records—who came into the club we were working. John Levy was on the road with us then.

This guy sent word back and said would I join his table, so John said to the waitress, "This is kind of a rough house around here, would you ask the gentleman to come back and see Mr. Shearing in his dressing room?" He was very nice about it.

Whether the message got through incorrectly or not at all I never knew, but we got an irate letter from this man saying if this is the way George Shearing and John Levy treat him when he comes into a club, he would see that no George Shearing record was played on any show that he had anything to do with.

This having happened in somewhat of a southern state, I guess John thought this character was trying to inject a racial issue. So he wrote a letter back in which he gave vent to some unusually strong statements. John isn't this kind of fellow, at all, but it infuriated him. Didn't this fellow realize, he wrote, that Mr.

Shearing was a blind man and that he, John Levy, was only trying to protect Mr. Shearing's welfare? If he didn't have the decency to come backstage and see Mr. Shearing, well then, as far as he, John Levy, was concerned, he could drop dead.

After this the man wrote back to MGM Records, for whom I was recording at the time. He was absolutely outraged at the tone of Levy's letter, he said. Where did that Jew think he got off?

Years later we went back to that same city and this same fellow was talking to our road manager, Ed Furst. He said, "You know something, Furst? George Shearing is one of the nicest people in the business, but I just can't stand that Jew, John Levy." What's doubly funny is not only that John Levy isn't Jewish, but that Ed Furst *is*.

One day I'm going to pay John's fare, take him down there and introduce him to that guy, who doesn't know to this day. I'd love to have somebody there with a camera to catch the double take. Not that I'd get it first hand, but I'd appreciate having somebody tell me how he looked.

Trixie Shearing: Back in the days when the late Billy Shaw was booking us, I had a letter from him stating that the concert we were supposed to do in California for Norman Granz had been canceled.

I called Billy and said, "Why?" and he wouldn't tell me at first.

I said, "Billy, there must be a reason. He's not allowed to cancel like that." So Billy said, "Well, to tell you the truth, Norman said he canceled it because George is anti-Semitic."

I said, "Billy, you know better than that," and he said, "I know, Trixie, but I couldn't convince him."

So I said, "Give me his number and let me talk to him." I called Norman long distance, and he made a lot of excuses. Finally I said, "Look, Norman, tell me the truth. I've known you too long not to be able to discuss this with you."

He said, "Billy Eckstine's manager came into a night club and heard George telling an anti-Semitic joke to a group at the table."

I started thinking back and it suddenly came to me. Obviously, Billy Eckstine's manager hadn't heard the story itself, or the punch line, but merely heard George's attempt to explain the punch line, which I remember he did in a very loud voice. George said, "Don't you get it? I don't want any Jews."

This was the story: During the war a very wealthy woman in Washington had planned to invite a group of young debutantes to her house to a dance; eligible young men in their circle being in short supply at the moment, she called up the local Army camp and said, "Please send me twelve soldiers, but I don't want any Jews."

On the night of the dance the doorbell rang and, when they opened the door, there were twelve Negro GIs standing on the steps. "Who are you?" stuttered the hostess. "I'm afraid there's been some mistake."

"No, ma'am," said one of the soldiers, "Sgt. Rosenbaum *never* makes a mistake."

Whitey Mitchell: You won't find the word "ofay" in your dictionary, but just about everybody who has heard of the word knows that it is used in reference to members of the so-called "white race." You could use the word Caucasian, but that isn't very accurate either. Ofay was originally a word of resentment used by Negroes only, and is simply the pig latin transposition of the word "foe". Nowadays, however, the word is used indiscriminately by both racial groups and, hopefully, has lost its original meaning.

Jerri Gray, a talented young dancer who used to be part of the jazz scene in New York, was seated at the bar in Joe Harbor's one day (that establishment is located directly across the street from Birdland, and is the logical successor to Charlie's Tavern), and took notice of me struggling through the door with my bass. She dispensed with me and my entire set of ancestors with the following line: "I don't mind ofays, but that Whitey Mitchell is overdoin' it."

•

Charlie Mingus offers his suggested name for a restaurant that should do a lot of business: Mammy's Kosher Pizzeria.

•

George Burns, during a TV interview with Steve Allen, said, "You may not know it, but years back I used to be part of an act called Delight and Davis. I used the name Sammy Davis. You know, *I* was Jewish before *he* was."

Herb Jeffries: Toward the end of the Los Angeles run of *Jump for Joy,* in which I played a featured role, John Garfield was brought in to groom the show for Broadway. The whole cast was introduced to Mr. Garfield and told he was going to make a lot of changes.

I was thrilled to meet him; he was a big movie star and I had heard he was a great liberal. He introduced himself to me and said, "Mr. Jeffries, as we all know, this is an all-Negro show, and the contrast between you and the other members of the cast is so great that I think it would be better for you to wear some dark make-up."

Well, I said okay, and the next night the make-up man plastered me with all this dark Egyptian make-up.

Duke Ellington had written the music and he and his whole band were in the pit playing the show. So I walked out to do my feature number with Dorothy Dandridge, *If Life Were All Peaches and Cream,* and I saw him look up at me. I kept feeling him staring a hole through me, and by this time I had forgotten that I had the make-up on and kept wondering what was wrong.

At the first intermission he came striding backstage, and he was mortified. He was furious.

"What in God's name are you trying to do?" he said. "Who do you think you are—Al Jolson?"

Well, as they say, this story has no moral, this story has no end —except, I guess, that even with my dark make-up we never did get to Broadway with *Jump for Joy.*

:

In 1948 Gene Norman hired Pat Willard, a teen-aged jazz fan, to handle publicity for a Billie Holiday concert he was promoting at Los Angeles' Shrine Auditorium. It was her first jazz promotion job and she was naively unprepared for the phone call she received from the entertainment editor of a prominent suburban newspaper.

"Pat," said the editor, "what color is Billie Holiday? I can't tell for sure from this mat you sent me, and you know, we don't run pictures of colored people."

Shocked almost speechless, Miss Willard said she didn't know and would have to ask Mr. Norman. Later she stood by while Norman called the editor and coolly informed him:

"The last time I saw Miss Holiday, sir, she was a lovely shade of soft purple with the most exquisite orange polka dots I've ever seen." With that, Norman gently hung up the phone.

The picture didn't run.

Los Angeles papers have changed since then, but not enough. In 1963 the same Miss Willard tried to place, in the two remaining local dailies, photos of the Modern Jazz Quartet prior to their appearance at Shelly's Manne Hole.

"We can't use this picture," said the representative of one paper. "They look like a bunch of Black Muslims."

Miss Willard then took the picture over to the other newspaper. "Sorry," she was told, "we do not support the beatnik movement."

"But John Lewis is no beatnik," protested Miss Willard. "In fact, he has even been criticized for being too restrained in manner, too dignified."

All the editor would say was, "If John Lewis ever shaves, you can bring a new picture of him."

As this book went to press, John Lewis had not shaved.

8

I invented jazz concerts!

by Prof. S. Rosentwig McSiegel

It is evidently known, beyond contradiction, that New Orleans is the cradle of jazz, and I, myself, happened to be the creator in the year 1901.

Jelly Roll Morton

● ● ● ● ● ● ● ●

A figure so legendary that he has been called a near-myth, Professor S. Rosentwig McSiegel began his literary career in 1940 in the long-forgotten pages of Swing Magazine. *His byline made medium-rare appearances in* Metronome *in the 1940s, and from the early 1950s was seen with welcome irregularity in* Down Beat. *He is said to have signed a recent agreement with* The Musical Courier *under the terms of which he guarantees to stay out of that publication for five years, with options.*

Professor McSiegel can truly claim that his story is, in essence, the story of jazz itself. As one of the foremost sousaphone players of the 1890s, he was among the first (and despite his innate modesty he will admit it under duress) to do everything. Since he has remained permanently under duress throughout his career as a chronicler of musical Americana, it was not without a considerable lack of diffidence that we approached him to reëdit, update and reissue some of his apocalyptic revelations.

:

(The jazz concert phenomenon was a landmark of the late 1940s and early 1950s. Symbolic of the era were the solos of exhibitionist tenor saxophonists such as Illinois Jacquet and Big Jay McNeely. Jacquet's work on How High The Moon *was a highlight of innumerable concerts presented by Norman Granz at Carnegie Hall, as were the percussion contests involving Buddy Rich and Gene Krupa. In the following memoir, Professor McSiegel relates how the jazz concert idea really began.)*

●

There are two schools of thought concerning the stage as a medium for the presentation of jazz. One school maintains that the concert hall has no place in jazz. The other, with equally valid and well-documented arguments, contends that jazz has no place in the concert hall.

Personally, I take a position squarely halfway between these two (like President Eisenhower, I have always cautioned against extremists on both sides). This places me about three blocks from Carnegie Hall and three blocks from Birdland.

The whole germ of the jazz concert concept germinated in prewar Germany. I was playing a four-hour location (with two two-hour options) at Max Ganzegasser's Konditorei und Brauhaus, just 19 miles from the heart of the Kurfuerstendamm on Route Sechsundsechzig.

The men in the band (I call them men because mankind is a generic term, though we had a girl on second trombone and I was never quite sure about the harpist) held the Konditorei in low esteem and nicknamed it "the Upholstered Sewer" (an irrational allegation, since the Konditorei actually was not upholstered). We used this spot as somewhere to sit down when times were slow, but this was one of our better years and we didn't spent more than about 47 weeks in the joint.

This being shortly after the Civil War, we called the group McSiegel's Illegal Eagles; appropriately, the whole thing began when we went on our first flying trip to Europe. We were operating under considerable transportation handicaps, since this was several decades before the official start of the aviation era; however, as some wag remarked at the time, "Nobody can stay high longer than those McSiegel cats." Our German tour was made under the auspices of the Jazz at the Philharmonic Foundation, on one of its Norman Grants.

Unfortunately communications were poor at the time and after losing contact with the foundation we found the bottom falling out of everything. After bumming around the Continent for a while, Pat O'Lipschitz having long since hocked his final fluegelhorn, we were soon flatter, if I may conjure up a colorful image momentarily, than Pat's high B Natural. So, necessity being the mother of all second rate gigs, that is how we wound up in Max's Konditorei.

Not having any horns, we worked there for a while as waiters, cooks and busboys. Pooling our tips, we then made a mass descent upon Fritz Mendelssohn's Schweinische Hockerei.

When we presented our claims it turned out there had been

some sort of mixup in the tickets. Our own instruments had been turned loose; in their place we received an unfamiliar assortment of horns and boxes. On showing them later to a group of more worldly musicians, we were told they consisted of three violins, two violas, a cello, an oboe, a bassoon and other arty artifacts.

"A fine thing!" commented Pat. "Here we are, the most modern jazz outfit west of the Rhine, and we wind up with a trunkful of longhair instruments. What can we," he continued, "do?"

Suddenly signals flashed in my head. One said: "Left turn on red light permitted," another "Right lane must turn left," a third "Do not pass Go." I pieced the signals together and found a brainstorm. "Why not take these longhair instruments into a longhair joint?" I suggested.

This was a crucial moment in jazz history. Only one obstacle presented itself: within a fifty-mile radius in both directions (up and down) there was no concert hall. But good old American know-how knew how to get back of this setback. We all set to work with beaver board, scissors and glue, and within three weeks had expanded the Konditorei into a municipal auditorium the like of which was never seen before or since; it was also the best ventilated (this only lasted a few months, until the roof was added).

We sent out invitations to friends and relations, announcing our opening day. Friends and our relations sent congratulations, but by an odd coincidence had all been called away that evening to an urgent business meeting, a grandmother's fit of gout or a conflicting concert in Cairo. Nevertheless, the word soon spread that we were planning a presentation of "Progressive Music" (a happy phrase coined by Wingy FitzGoldberg, who had just joined us on phallic cymbals). This billing for our brand of music turned out to be singularly apt, since at every concert the group sounded progressively worse.

Nevertheless, we took in enough marks (and don't forget, these were not Confederate marks) to pay our way back home, whereupon we decided to return to a simple, unpretentious small-band jazz format for a while, to play in simple, unattended clubs. But fate decreed otherwise. Somebody up at the Gloe Jazzer Agency got two contracts mixed up—ours and the New York Philharmonic's—and we found ourselves booked into Carnegie Hall, while the New York Philharmonic played an off-night at the Village Gate.

When the truth leaked out, the Carnegie operators were nice about it. They made a few slight new stipulations in our contract (something about guaranteeing to reupholster all torn seats), but this didn't faze us, and as the great day drew near we worked up a promotional campaign second to nothing.

First we blanketed the city with disc jockey plugs. (The night we did this was so stormy that we wound up with a truckload of wet blankets.) Pat arranged to start his own show, 15 minutes every Tuesday from 5:30 to 5:45 a.m. over WWWW in Montauk, Long Island. I personally guested, all in a single day, on *Breakfast with Benny, Brunch in the Bronx, Luncheon at Luchow's, Tea in Teaneck, Dinner with Dinah* and *Supper with Symphony Sid* (Sid at this time was barely out of his teens and, like radio itself, was in a primitive stage of development). After this round of shows, by midnight I realized that I would need a new tux for the concert, six inches larger around the waist.

Needless to say, with publicity of this magnitude we could hardly miss. Yet the Cassandras of the music business (including even Sam Cassandra, whom I considered a friend) predicted dire results. "Jazz in Carnegie Hall?" they said. "We predict dire results. The hall will be half empty." They had to eat their words, of course, when the curtain rose and revealed that Carnegie was half-*full*.

The sensation of the concert was a young tenor man named Jack Coates who had just breezed in from Chicago. We called him "Chicago" Coates. Since we couldn't expect to fill Carnegie with the type of cats who would patronize us at Kelly's Stable we told Chicago not to play for the cats, but to put on the dog a little. Accordingly, he played notes only a dog could hear, inventing a concerto for steam-whistle entitled *The Firefly and the Gnome,* which later, under the abbreviated title *Fly 'n' Gnome,* was swiped by another tenor player, who shall be gnomeless.

I need hardly tell you that Coates had the audience eating

out of his hand (he was selling peanuts, popcorn and candy during intermission). After the break came a somewhat esoteric interlude, a set of quadrilles and French-Canadian folk songs by a pianist we had sneaked across the border, Peter Oscarson; but the limited appeal of Oscarson was happily canceled out as all through his set one of our drummers, the charming Jean Cooper, was fighting for possession of the percussion equipment while our other drum specialist, the belligerent Rudy Beach, was insisting that it was he who was supposed to accompany Oscarson. This custody fight ended with Cooper and Beach each holding one wire brush, one stick, half a bass drum and half a snare. I need hardly add that this was the origin of one of my most-imitated innovations, the drum battle.

Since our first night produced the first and biggest gross ever attracted up to that time by a jazz concert at Carnegie, we decided that a crowd of this kind was too good to lose. Accordingly, we initiated a course in audience manners. After three months of instruction in such niceties as how to spit at the stage, how to talk loud enough to cover up the music, how to tear chairs without leaving fingerprints, and even how to stub out one's cigarette on the neck of the guy in the row in front, our students emerged perfectly equipped to be a jazz audience.

After the success of Chicago Coates had gone to his pants and he had become too big for his britches, we replaced him with "Big Foot" McMealy, originator of the so-called "McMealy Mouthed" school of tenor sax. There may be indignant denials from others who claim the honor, but I can truthfully boast that Big Foot, while working with me, became the first man to take off his shirt during his tenor solo *without* removing his jacket. Later, as his musicianship improved, he learned to take off his socks without removing his shoes, and to take off his mouthpiece while removing his teeth.

Big Foot's big hit was *Hoo Hoo the Moo,* adapted by my old buddy Sing Bum Sing from a tender Chinese folk song. Later he scored an even bigger success with *Perdoodoo,* the first 69 choruses of which he played while standing on his head. When the novelty of Joe's musical inversion wore off we introduced an extra gimmick: he remained upside down, but his head was on a small record player on the floor, stage left, that revolved at 33⅓, the spindle fitting neatly into the crater in Joe's cranium.

Later, when our audience tired of this, we had the cavity enlarged to accomodate a doughnut sized spindle so that he could revolve at 45 r.p.m. By this time *Perdoodoo* was old hat and he was featuring such novelties as *Voodoo, Hoodoo* and *Yoodoo,* all based on a revolutionary idea I had dreamed up: the chord changes of *I Got Rhythm.*

I need hardly tell you how our pioneering efforts ended. Within a few years everybody and his brother (including his brother Irving) was making money out of jazz concerts, while here am I, patiently waiting, looking for a gig for New Year's Eve. It's like I always said: originality pays off, but usually to some other guy.

9

For bass faces only

How on earth do you get that thing under your chin?

Leonard F. Larson

● ● ● ● ● ● ● ●

Whitey Mitchell: Most people cannot resist the temptation to comment humorously on the plight of the bass player carrying his bass to or from work. Each person seems to think that his is a highly original and amusing remark, but any bass player can tell you that all of these hilarious observations derive from a single, ancient chestnut, to wit: "Why didn't you take up the piccolo?"

My brother, Red Mitchell, says there are four clichés normally addressed to bass players. They run approximately as follows:

"What have you got in there, your grandmother?"

"How on earth do you get that thing under your chin?"

"Isn't that an awful big load for a little fellow like you?" (You can be 6'4" and they'll still throw this line at you.)

"What kind of vitamin pills have you been feeding that fiddle?"

There are, however, a few original souls left in the world, and there is a woman in California eminently qualified to be included in this category. She spotted Red struggling to get to a record date with the bass and immediately invoked: "Well, when you get where you're going, I certainly hope they ask you to play."

Shorty Sherock: I was in Ben Pollack's band, and there was Fazola and a bass player named Thurman Teague. We were traveling with Thurman, who had his own car, but Sammy Taylor, who was the drummer, and Harry James, who was in the trumpet section, were driving the truck to make a few extra bucks. We were all making around $60 or $65 a week with Pollack.

We left Nashville after the job, around 2 a.m., and Harry and Sammy Taylor had been to a jam session and were taking care of the band truck—you know, putting the heavier instruments on the bottom, and the drums on top of that, and then on top of that, the bass violin, which was carried in an oilskin sack.

We got into Memphis about 7 or 8 a.m., and we checked into this apartment hotel. About an hour later we got a call from Harry James, asking to speak to Thurman.

"We had a little accident," he says. "The truck rolled over into the ditch, and I think there's a little damage to your bass."

"How serious does it look?" said Thurman, in the manner of a mother whose child had been hurt.

"Better come and see for yourself."

So Thurman got in a cab and went down to where they have the truck. It was a complete shambles. It had rolled over three or four times. And all the instruments on the bottom had rolled over onto the bass. Well, Thurman came back into the hotel room holding the only solid piece of the whole thing that was left—just the long neck of the bass fiddle. He unbuttoned the case and little matchsticks of wood fell out—nothing but shreds. The whole thing was completely pulverized.

Thurman was in tears. "It's an old, antique Italian bass," he says. "It's worth so much money. Do you think I could have it fixed?"

André Previn: When Red Mitchell and Frank Capp and I used to go on the road, it used to be possible to put the bass fiddle in a special case the airlines provided and place it in the baggage compartment and pay overweight on it.

A couple of years ago the airlines made a new ruling about it, which strikes me as strange in the first place, because you wouldn't think it would be that commonplace an occurrence. The rule was that you could no longer carry the bass as baggage; you had to buy a ticket for it. And put it on the seat.

It's an expensive joke, because you're a trio and suddenly you're traveling as a quartet. This gave rise first of all to the obvious jokes, because they always have to be made out to a specific name, so it would be traveling as Mr. Sam Bass or Mr. Max Bass, or whatever.

But, the first time it happened I paid for the bass and had the ticket for it, and the farther the plane went the more we brooded about this and the more angry we became. We decided to get even with the airline.

In a sort of childish retrogression we said: all right, the bass has a ticket in its own name, we demanded—and got!—the extra drinks, the extra lunch, the whole works. We had them all brought to the bass; after all, if its fare was paid, why shouldn't it be treated as a regular passenger like the rest of us?

Tommy Gumina: Irving Edelman once played bass for Joe Venuti. Joe drove him nuts with one gag he played on him. He started putting a little bag of sand in Irving's bass every night, and the instrument gradually kept getting heavier and heavier.

Finally Irving went up to Venuti one night and told him he was going to quit, because all that heavy Italian food and wine they'd have after work each night was getting him so out of shape he could barely carry his bass anymore.

Joe finally had to explain the gag or lose a bass player.

Gerald Wilson: I was playing trumpet in Jimmie Lunceford's band. Around 1940 we had a date at the Paramount Theater on Times Square; that was when they always had a big feature movie and a long stage show with a name band.

The band always worked from a big pit, as wide as the stage. During the movie it was kept way down below the level of the orchestra seats. But as the show began, while the members of the band sat in the pit, it would rise slowly for a full half minute or so, maybe ten feet or so altogether, until it was so high that if you were sitting in the front row you'd have to really crane your neck to catch a glimpse of the band.

Well, one day as the first show began, Mose Allen got in the pit a little late, and maybe he wasn't in his regular place. And as the whole area slowly rose from the depths, there was a strange crunching sound coming from the area of the rhythm section.

We turned toward the sound and were horrified to see Mose's bass fiddle caught between the pit and the stage, being slowly and helplessly crushed to pieces.

By the time we were all the way up on the elevator-stage, poor Mose had nothing left but four strings and a rather large pile of wood. But it was hard to resist the temptation to congratulate him on his good fortune. After all, suppose Mose and the bass had changed places?

10

Hi-Fi fable II: Double jeopardy

by Leonard Feather and Jack Tracy

• • • • • • •

It sounded like a crazy idea.

I mean, anybody could have thought of it, but, like, some cats just don't *bother* to think.

The thing is, you've got to be hip enough to get around your limitations, and not get hung up with them.

Anyway, by the time I got out of school and started making some gigs with the cats who were getting steady work, it wasn't long before some people began talking. I wasn't giving Dizzy or Miles any trouble, but when a few of the other hornmen in town began to fall by and listen, I knew I must be blowing pretty good.

Oh, I knew where I was weak. First of all, I didn't have the chops to get 'way upstairs—the middle of the horn felt better. And I didn't have all the fingers some cats do, so I would just kind of coast over the changes, you know what I mean?

Well, this one night Rudy Burns came through town, and after they finished their gig at the Downbeat he fell by our joint for a taste. I'd already finished playing, but somebody must have told him something about me, because when we were introduced he said, "I've heard some good things about you, man. Maybe you'll be ready for us one of these days."

Now when Rudy Burns says something like that to you, man, you just don't take it lightly. Even if you play third chair with him for awhile, you've got it made. His music may not be everybody's dish of tea, but, man, he wins all those polls, and makes all those overseas trips, and gets all those record gigs, and has his picture in *Playboy* every couple of issues. Stuff like that rubs off on anybody who works in the band even for a little while. So that compliment from him was like Ralph Houk saying he'd like to have you on his ball club. And let me tell you, I wasn't going to let him forget it.

But he didn't say anymore. He didn't give me his card or tell me to look him up the next time I was in New York (which, truthfully, would be the first time). But you know what the grapevine is like in this business. It wasn't more than three months later that I was playing a gig in Springfield and the alto player, Al Fisher (he worked with Kenton for about three months one time), said, "They tell me Rudy Burns is looking for a good trumpet man."

"How *good* would good be?"

"Well, man, you know Rudy. If his section don't hit like four high Cs every eight bars he figures they must be cacked out. Remember Cat Anderson the night we heard Duke? Well, Rudy's horns are supposed to sound like a whole litter of Cats. Don't take this personal, but I hope you didn't think I meant *you* should try to get the gig."

"Al, my man," I said, "with your help I believe I *can* get that gig. And that bread. And I will not even have to make a live audition. If you will give me some assistance, Al, we will both make a handsome taste."

I explained the scene to him at a quiet bar after the gig. "You will receive 25 percent of my first three months' earnings if I keep the job," I told him, "or exactly half of everything I make if I get fired sooner. All I want is some of your technical aid."

Al, not being one to turn down a found dollar or two, agreed readily when he heard my scam.

The first thing we did the next morning was to find a pawn shop that had a bass trumpet for sale cheap. We had to go to three before we found one. Our next stop was Al's hotel room, where he kept his tape recorder. His end was simple—he took care of the machine, I took care of the music.

First he recorded at 7½ inches per second while I made a modest little speech that went something like: "Mr. Burns, I hope you won't mind my imposing on your time this way, and I trust you don't mind my doing an audition with a play-along record, but I'd like you to listen to a couple of little things to give you an idea of how I'm coming along."

Then Al switched the machine to 3¾ inches per second—half speed—and I picked up the bass trumpet. "Now play the *Can't*

Get Started accompaniment at half-speed, Al," I instructed. Then I started to blow.

A chorus-and-a-half did it. I played a lot of double-time, which was easy at this tempo, and ended with a flashy bass trumpet high note, also easy. Then we did *Indiana,* at one of those kind of medium, finger-popping grooves, and I must say I did get a little tricky. It was going to sound like something else when we got through.

Then we played them back—at 7½ speed. You know, it even amazed me?! Everything came out an octave higher, which brought it up from bass trumpet to regular trumpet register. I play with almost no vibrato, so we didn't have the nanny-goat problem. The double-time on *Started* sounded like Diz on one of his fantastic nights. I was really quite proud.

It felt so good we decided to add one more, a chorus of *All The Things You Are.* When we finished, Al gave me a grin and said, "I'll bet you're going to fool the old bastard with this thing at that. Let's go mail it to him."

"Splendid idea," I agreed. "And if Rudy ever has an opening in his sax section, remember, I never forget a friend."

Man, it worked like a charm. Exactly 32 hours later, Rudy called me from New York. "They told me you were pretty good," he said, "but I had no idea! I only had to hear the first number on that tape you sent! I'm sending you air fare. Be at Nola's for a rehearsal by two in the afternoon Monday."

Naturally I didn't expect to hold the gig very long. But if I could bluff my way through by saying I hadn't worked enough lately to keep my chops in top shape, that might get me through a few weeks and let me put that "Formerly With Rudy Burns" after my name.

But that's not quite the way it worked out.

Oh, I made it through the first rehearsal pretty good. I read the charts o.k., and I knew Rudy wouldn't give me any solos right away because that would have caused a scene with the other cats in the section who were veterans with the band. Everything was working out pretty much on schedule.

But that same night the band played a night club just outside

Newark. About halfway through intermission the bandboy came up to me at the bar and said, "The old man wants to see you in the dressing room."

The first thing I saw when I went into the room was the tape recorder on the cot.

"Cigaret?" said Burns.

"No, thanks, skipper, just put one out."

"I just had time to listen to the whole tape you sent me," he said. "Why don't we hear it together so we can figure out how to really feature you in this band."

"Why, thank you," I said, "but why don't we wait until the band gets used to me, and my chops get straight?"

"No, no; I want to start making use of the talent we have in the section right away." He sounded very sincere, and I figured it was just the blue smoke floating past his eyes that made them look so cold.

He hit the "Play" button on the machine, and I will have to admit that it sounded the end. *Can't Get Started* was a gas. I mean, you just don't hear something like that every day. *Indiana* was like somebody had crossed a Gillespie with a Mendez and the offspring was a hungry tiger. I had to lower my eyes in pride.

Then Burns played *All The Things You Are*. And I must confess that it was great, too—right up until five seconds after the end. It was then that you could hear Al's voice say, "I'll bet you're going to fool the old bastard with this thing, at that. Let's go mail it to him."

What Al said didn't really bug Burns. In fact, I don't think that Burns even figured out what Al said. It was the *way* he said it that had me out on my can before my first night with the Rudy Burns band was finished with.

You see, when Al talked, he sounded just like Donald Duck.

11

How long the hair

Shostakovitch small by a waterfall . . .

Hugo Friedhofer

• • • • • • • •

Billy Taylor: Once there was a symphony conductor who fell in love with a certain contemporary symphony, but for years refused to perform it because one of the movements had to be played by a jazz pianist.

"I won't have it," he insisted. "I've heard about jazz musicians. They're drunks, dope fiends, unreliable, sloppy, can't read music —I wouldn't hire one."

Finally, however, he was persuaded by the orchestra manager to try the work at a rehearsal and he, the manager, would provide a capable pianist.

At precisely 15 minutes before the rehearsal the pianist came in, slim, quiet, dressed impeccably by Brooks Brothers, a rolled black umbrella hanging from his left forearm, a New York *Times* in his right hand.

He sat down inconspicuously and read the *Times.* When it was time for him to play he walked confidently to the piano and sight-read the score brilliantly, improvising marvelously when it was so indicated.

Finished, he sat down again. When the entire work was finished the maestro ran to him, shook his hand warmly, begged his forgiveness for any misconceptions the maestro might have had about jazz musicians. "Another rehearsal Thursday," he said to the pianist, "then we perform the work Friday at Carnegie Hall."

Thursday's rehearsal was an even greater success. The pianist, now familiar with the work, played with incredible impact.

Again the maestro congratulated him and shook his hand. "Tomorrow you will be superb at Carnegie Hall," he exclaimed. "The reviews will be sensational!"

"Yeah, well, I wanted to talk to you about that," said the pianist. "You see, tomorrow night I've got another gig, and I'll have to send you a sub."

122

André Previn: Otto Klemperer, the great German conductor, came to New York, and he wanted to find out how his recordings, on Angel Records, were doing.

One of the men connected with Angel Records at that time was a fellow named Mendelssohn. He took Klemperer in tow and they went to a big local store and asked for Klemperer's record of the Beethoven Seventh.

The clerk looked through his stock and he said: "No, we have Fritz Reiner's, Eugene Ormandy's and Bruno Walter's."

The Angel Records man naturally was embarrassed. "You're sure you don't have Klemperer's?"

"No, we don't," said the clerk. "But I don't understand. These others are so great, why would you be interested in Otto Klemperer's?"

"I'll tell you why, young man," said Klemperer. "If you want to know the truth, I happen to be Otto Klemperer."

"Sure," said the clerk, "you're Otto Klemperer. And I suppose the guy with you is Beethoven."

"No," said Klemperer, "He's Mendelssohn."

:

There's a famous story about Jascha Heifetz's debut at Carnegie when he was around thirteen. It was one of the legendary debuts of all time; the whole town went to pieces over him. And at the debut were several other famous violinists including Mischa Elman, and Moriz Rosenthal, the pianist.

Half an hour or so after the recital had started, Mischa Elman turned to Rosenthal and said "God, it's hot in here!"

And Rosenthal said: "Not for pianists!"

:

When Frank Sinatra first became the idol of the bobby soxers he had a press agent, the late George Evans, who had the reputation of being one of the world's greatest and most ingenious public relations men.

Frank had just scored that first incredible success at the New York Paramount, and he was coming out to the West Coast. George wanted some kind of enormous publicity thing for his arrival here.

It happened that Sir Thomas Beecham was in town to conduct the Los Angeles Philharmonic and Evans made an appointment with Beecham, explained who he was,—the manager of a singer called Frank Sinatra. Beecham said he had never heard of him. So Evans explained what an enormous success he was, the idol of millions of people. "Mr. Sinatra is arriving tomorrow, on the Super Chief, and he's going to get out in Pasadena to avoid the screaming mobs that will be at Union Station, and we think it would be a marvelous thing, Sir Thomas, if you were to meet him."

And Beecham said: "Meet him in Pasadena? Why should I? The blighter didn't come to meet me when I got to New York!"

:

Beecham used to hate to rehearse well known pieces of repertoire. One day he had gone through a perfunctory rehearsal with whatever orchestra he was conducting, and he said: "Look, gentlemen, we are also going to play the first Brahms; but I know you've all played it many, many times, and I've certainly conducted it often enough; there aren't that many peculiarities in it, so let's not rehearse it, let's approach it fresh tonight, you just watch me carefully and we'll have a wonderful performance, I'm sure."

He started to walk off, at which point one of the clarinet players raised his hand, and said: "Sir Thomas, forgive me; I am a substitute clarinet player, I'm not with this orchestra usually; and I'm embarrassed to tell you this, but I have never in my life played the first Brahms."

"You've never played it at all?"

"No, sir."

Beecham thought a moment and said: "Well, my boy, you'll love it," and walked off.

Johnny Guarnieri: Did you hear about the time Jascha Heifetz was doing a radio program in a New York studio?

He and his accompanist want to catch the elevator up to the studio. Heifetz was carrying his violin in its case. The conversation went something like this:

Elevator Operator: "I'm sorry, but we can't take you up. Musicians are supposed to take the freight elevator with their instruments."

Accompanist: "But don't you know who this is? This gentleman is the world's foremost violinist!"

Elevator Operator: "Listen, I don't care if he's Rubinoff—he'll still have to take the freight!"

•

One of the wittiest and most talented men in Hollywood is David Raksin. Though best known as composer of *Laura*, he first came to prominence in the 1930s when he arranged the score of the Chaplin film *Modern Times*.

Philadelphia-born, Raksin studied at the University of Pennsylvania. "Dave Hass was assistant to Howard Lanin when we gigged in a band together," he recalls. "Once we had a New Year's Eve job for which Dave had to front the band. He was delighted to have the job, but perhaps it rattled him a little, because at one point he turned to the band and beat us off this way:

"One, two, *Tiger Rag!*"

:

About ten days before graduation Raksin learned that he would have to take an instrumental examination that involved playing a concert work on clarinet.

"There was no time to work up a Mozart concerto or anything like that," he recalls, "so I just wrote myself a piece; it was full of what were actually jazz runs, and easy on the fingers. I got some old yellow manuscript and wrote it on that to make it look authentic.

"I got Harl McDonald, the head of the department, to play piano for me; he was in on the gag and so were a lot of the student body. The man I had to get past on this exam was a professor of esthetics named Paul Krummeich, who thought I was much too fresh anyhow and probably would have loved to flunk me.

"But we got in there and we wowed them. I was too young and dumb to know about fear, so I went in and played this thing and passed; but the punch line came when McDonald went up to this fellow and asked him: 'How did you like the performance?'

" 'Well,' shrugged Krummeich, 'I've heard it played better.' "

:

Not long after his song *Laura* first hit, Raksin was invited by the publicist Adeline Hanson to an interview on a small radio station in Glendale. Raksin heard the tune being played on a turntable in the control room and saw a couple of girls in the booth rapping on the window as if to draw his attention to it.

The engineer, his curiosity piqued, came out of the booth and said to Raksin, "You have something to do with that song?"

"Oh, yes."

"Which, the words or the music?"

"The music."

"Oh," said the engineer, "you must be Harold Arlen."

"No," said Raksin, "I'm Johnny Mercer."

:

When Raksin first went to New York he worked in an extraordinary band directed by Al Goodman. The personnel included Dick McDonough, Tommy Dorsey, Miff Mole and Oscar Levant.

At one point during a rehearsal Al Goodman became very angry and started criticizing the orchestra.

"Look," said Levant, "you'd better cut that out or I'll follow your beat."

:

Some of Levant's sardonic remarks have become classics. Here are some samples of his ad libs during the time he conducted a TV show in Hollywood a few years ago.

"Ralph Edwards wanted to do my life . . . but he couldn't find any friends."

"My doctor told me it was dangerous to watch the Dinah Shore program as I have a tendency to diabetes."

"I'm a controversial person. My friends either dislike me or hate me."

"I'm like Eisenhower. Once I make up my mind I'm full of indecision."

"Who needs Disneyland? I've got fantasies of my own."

:

Raksin worked with Levant on a picture called *Nothing Sacred*. When terms were being arranged for Levant to compose the music, David Selznick brusquely asked him: "On how little a week can you live?"

"I won't work for that!" snapped Levant.

:

Levant was a protege of Arnold Schoenberg, who really was fond of him, treating him as his own private bad boy. One day Levant and Raksin went to visit Schoenberg. At one point the composer's son, Ronnie, entered the room looking just like old man Schoenberg.

His father stopped him, reached into a window seat, picked up tiny violin case, pulled out a quarter size violin, tuned it up and handed it to the child without a word.

The youngster gave a despairing look, and started to play what Raksin describes as "the most incredible junk we ever heard." The old man looked up proudly and said, "You see? He improvises all the time!"

"It took us two whole days," Raksin recalls, "to realize that Schoenberg had been putting us on."

:

On another occasion Raksin went for a lesson with Schoenberg.

"The old man was very interested in my movie work; it was not his world, but he dug it. I guess I looked kind of green around the edges and he said in that high, fluty voice of his, 'Vot are you doink now?'

" 'I've just been assigned to a picture about airplanes,' I said.

"Now, when you talk to a music teacher, you talk in terms of examples. So he looked at me for a moment and he said, 'You vill not find an example in Schubert.'

"We had one of our long, long lessons, about two hours, and he was seeing me out the door when he suddenly says, as if nothing had happened in between:

" 'Like bees, only bigger.' "

:

Hugo Friedhofer, a remarkable composer, is well known in Hollywood as a wit and inveterate punster. He is also known for his vitriolic tongue, but Raksin recalls one period when he remained quite placid for a long while. Finally, though, at a meeting, he let fly at some helpless fellow writer, tore him to verbal shreds and left the pieces lying around the table. He ended up pointing directly at Raksin, looking as though he now wanted to take off on another victim. But Raksin quieted him with a single deftly delivered shaft.

"Hugo," he said gently, "somebody has been putting umbrage in your Miltown."

:

Several composers were holding a meeting to draw up a series of contract proposals for a group of producers.

"Since we were relatively new at this sort of thing," says Raksin, "we were appalled at the amount of verbiage involved. Surrounding clauses, sub-clauses and what-not; it was all too much for us.

"It got longer and longer, and we were looking at it in a state of depressed confusion, when at last one composer, Jeff Alexander, came up with a suggestion.

"Why don't we," he said, "just give them the chord symbols?"

:

Once at the Fox studios Raksin was ribbed by a couple of secretaries who kidded him about the fact that the picture on which they were working was successfully dispensing with all music.

"Why," asked Raksin, "do the producer and the director feel this picture should be without music?"

"It all takes place on a lifeboat," said one girl, "and it's way out on the ocean, so where could the music come from?"

Raksin said: "You just go and ask Mr. Hitchcock where the camera comes from, and I'll tell him where the music comes from!"

:

In 1962 Raksin had a memorable meeting with Igor Stravinsky. He had promised to bring something over to Stravinsky's house, but admits to having had an ulterior motive: he wanted his little boy, Alexander, to meet the old man.

They went over and found Stravinsky in rare form. "He was enchanted with Alexander," says Raksin. "First he kissed his hands, then his nose, then his feet; and all the time we were talking he had the baby's foot in his hand.

"At one point he turned to the baby and said, 'This is a lot more fun than being 80 years old, right?'

"Later I told Stravinsky that I know now exactly what is going to happen with Alexander.

"Some day, many years from now, when *Symphony of the Psalms* has become like a Bach B Minor Mass, they'll be playing it in college, and Alexander will get up and say, 'I used to know that man, and he kissed my foot.' And the teacher will say, 'Stop talking nonsense, shut up and sit down!' "

12

How I caught music red-handed

by Prof. S. Rosentwig McSiegel

I have here in my hand documentary proof that there are eleven card-carrying Communists in the Moscow Symphony Orchestra.

Sen. Phineas MacAbre

● ● ● ● ● ● ● ●

(Prof. McSiegel unburdened himself of the following observations during the darkest days of the McCarthy reds-under-the-beds era.)

Ed. Note: The opinions expressed by Prof. McSiegel do not necessarily reflect his views. As we recall with gratitude when we read each platitude, he was given the widest latitude to express his attitude.

For many years now I have been perturbed by a situation that has been working its way insidiously into the music business and has now reached the proportions of a national menace.

I am not one to seek sensational headlines, so I will put it as mildly as possible: THE COMMUNISTS ARE TAKING OVER THE MUSIC BUSINESS!

The situation has all the earmarx of a trend, and the trend is not yet at an end, my friend. So, in order to combat it, I have organized the McSiegel Investigation of American Subversive Musical Activities, which for brevity I shall call MIASMA.

As we all know, the country is in a dangerous state today. The American eagle is flying with a left and a right wing, while every red-blooded American knows that two right wings are all it needs. Nowhere is this more evident than in the ranks of the AFM, whose members actually boast that jazz musicians enjoy "freedom of expression." This phrase is a devious cover-up for the flaunting, through music, of all kinds of dangerously individual radical ideas without submitting first to scripting, screening and scrutiny, the three musts for all public utterances, whether musical or verbal, in an organized society.

With this in mind, MIASMA has secured the services of Senator Phineas MacAbre, the man who is doing more than any American to save the country from enlightened conservatism. Senator MacAbre and I just sent our two ace emissaries, Pat O'Lipschitz and Wingy FitzGoldberg, on a fact-foundering tour. They returned with a welter, nay a spate, of facts on which to build the MIASMA Code.

Here, briefly, is our plan:

(1) All members of the AFM are to submit immediately to a loyalty oath, pledging allegiance to Senator MacAbre and the principles for which he stands, as well as to that great ex-musician and fighting anti-liberal, State Senator Jack Tenney of California; to Westbrook Lewis Jr., Gerald L.K. McCormick and Upton Hopper. Those who take the oath will be allowed to continue their membership, provided all music is submitted on manuscript before performance, and cleared by MIASMA.

The above rule will not apply to obvious unhealthy elements, who will be erased from membership without trial, since they are obviously guilty of harboring thoughts. These include Red Norvo, who operates a small cell right in his own trio (he has Red Mitchell on bass); Red Rodney, Red Nichols, Red Allen, and Red Buttons. The last pair are doubly guilty, since their hair is black and gray, respectively, and thus they do not even have the flimsy excuse of pigmentation to justify their fellow-traveling nicknames.

(2) All key figures in the industry will be called to a special hearing, and will bring with them all phonograph records made by them (a) during the New Deal, (b) during or since the Nazi-Soviet pact, (c) during the recording ban.

These hearings are expected to uncover a plethora, nay a glut, of subversive situations. A casual glance at the records of a few top leaders, as inspected by Pat and Wingy, revealed the following:

Woody Herman—Big record hit recently was *Jump In The Line* —a not-too-subtle attempt to corral converts for the party. Also was playing *Red Top* extensively during the mid-'40s.

Stan Kenton—Has been trading for years on the term "progressive"—always a euphemism for dangerous radical activity.

Duke Ellington—Played a concert for Russian War Relief at Carnegie Hall in 1943, and at that time was overheard by three overhearers referring to Russia as "our ally."

Count Basie—Was at one time assiduously plugging a composition titled *Red Bank Boogie*, a flagrant plea for nationalization

133

of our banks, a form of creeping socialism that cannot but lead to crawling communism.

Benny Goodman—Was responsible for recording and popularizing *Down South Camp Meeting,* clearly an invitation to a conclave calculated to excite racial tensions in Dixie; Goodman, himself a homeless cosmopolitan, has inflamed these tensions further by using numerous racially-tense musicians in his bands through the years.

And so forth through the entire list of name bandleaders. Are you beginning to appreciate now that it's time for a change?

(3) All songs written by Tin Pan Alley for public consumption are to be sent to the MIASMA censorship bureau. Had this system been introduced years ago, we might have saved the public from being subverted by such dangerous doctrines as *Red Sails In The Sunset* (Where did he sail? Why did he wait until he could leave under cover of darkness?), Charlie Parker's *Red Cross* (a barbarous assault on Christianity) and George Wallington's *Red White and Blue,* in which with fiendish subtlety the true intent is covered up by the inclusion of two other colors; also *Pinky* (why did Sarah Vaughan record this? What was Ethel Waters doing in the movie?), and *Pink Elephants* (where do they go for their sources of material, the Moscow Zoo?).

I hope you can see from the above brief sketch of our plans that MIASMA will perform a sterling, nay a trojan, service for the music world. After we are through we shall have a smaller, compacter music business, free of undesirable elements, in which the red corpuscles will have been removed from our bloodstream; the yellow streak, the white feather and the blue funk will provide the colors for our proud new national flag.

Three cheers for the yellow, white and blue!

13

The night-blooming jazzmen

Golf is tougher than oboe.

Dave Barbour

• • • • • • • •

André Previn: Years ago during a visit to New York I went to Birdland, alone. I was sitting there in the dark and it was kind of a gloomy scene altogether.

A man came over and sat down next to me. Slowly, as he sat there silently, his head nodded forward, and gradually he keeled over and suddenly he was asleep on my shoulder. Well, far be it from me to disturb someone's sleep; I just let him lie there.

At the end of the set, one of the fellows from the bandstand, I think it was Sweets Edison, came over and started laughing.

"André," he said, "have you ever met Bud Powell?"

"No," I said, "but of course I'd love to."

"Easy to arrange. He's sleeping on you!"

•

Soupy Sales tells the story of a tall, handsome physician who bore a remarkable resemblance to a celebrated singer.

On arrival in Detroit from a small town in Missouri, to attend a convention, he was greeted at the airport by a skycap: "Pardon me, but aren't you Joe Williams? I saw you when you were with Basie's band and I'm one of your biggest fans."

"No," was the reply, "I'm Dr. Martin Johnson and I'm here to attend a convention."

A few minutes later, as he stepped into a taxi, the cab-driver stopped him with: "Joe Williams! What are you doing in town? I've got all your records and—"

"I'm sorry, I'm not Joe Williams. My name is Martin Johnson and I'm going to a medical convention."

As he entered the hotel and prepared to check in, the desk clerk observed: "Sweets Edison still playing with you, Mr. Williams? That was a fine album you made . . ."

Wearily, the doctor explained his identity again.

Finally he reached his hotel room—or what he thought was his room, though as the door opened he was greeted by a tall, stunningly beautiful girl dressed in a flimsy negligee.

"Why, Joe Williams!" said the girl. "What are *you* doing here?"

Without a moment's hesitation, the answer came in a full, resonant baritone:

"Every day . . . . . every day I have the blues. . . . ."

Mike Gould: When Eddie Condon was in the hospital, his brother, Pat, and I used to visit him a lot, mainly to get something to eat. His room was always full of fruit and candy that people had sent, and neither Pat nor myself had a job.

One day Eddie gave us a five dollar bill and asked us to please call his sister in Providence, Rhode Island, to tell her everything was o.k. and that he wasn't going to die. So Pat and I went to a hardware store and bought about fifteen cents worth of quarter-sized slugs—this was around 1936, before they had outlawed slugs. Then we went over to the Lincoln hotel, where Tommy Dorsey was working. We figured with the money we'd save by using the slugs we could have a few drinks and a few laughs and maybe see a movie on 42nd Street.

As we walked into the hotel with this pocketful of slugs, I suddenly had an idea. "Let's wait until six o'clock, when the telephone rates change." So we saved a few slugs as well as the loot.

:

One night Dave Tough and I were backstage at a Tommy Dorsey hotel job and one of the younger musicians came up to us somewhat excitedly and said, "Dave, why don't you come out front? Vincent Lopez just came in and Tommy's talking to him. Don't you want to meet him?"

Dave thought for a minute, then said, "Well, if he looks anything like *Nola* sounds, no, I don't want to meet him."

:

One thing Wild Bill Davison had besides his trumpet was a fabulous wardrobe, including a tuxedo, tails—the works. One night—this goes back to around 1933—there were about four of us in his hotel room on the second floor, and he was planning to sneak out because he was broke.

So each of us put two or three suits on, plus hats and topcoats, dropped some luggage out of the window, and walked out of the hotel, hoping they wouldn't get wise.

A week or so later I ran into Bill, and he said, "Thanks for helping me out of that hotel, Mike. But I just found out I still had three days to go on the money I had down in advance."

:

After Irving Goodman, Benny Goodman's trumpeter brother, saw *The Benny Goodman Story* movie, I asked him how he liked it. "The only thing about it that was true was the address on the mail box in Chicago," he said.

:

Joe Reichman was a society bandleader who played piano and always wore white tails.

He used to have a gimmick, on stage shows anyway, where he had a narrow trough in the piano just above the keyboard. There was an electric element in it like in a toaster, and before each show he'd put a special powder in. Then when he played *Smoke Gets In Your Eyes,* he'd press a button, the element would heat up, and gentle smoke would float around.

Well, there was a comic on the bill who had to follow this bit, and it really bugged him. He'd have to come on to a stage that was full of smoke, and the audience would still be talking about the gimmick instead of listening to him, and so he decided to do something about it.

He got some of the cheapest, dirtiest tobacco he could find, mixed it all up with some cigaret loads—you know, those things that you put in the ends of cigarets—and filled up the trough with it.

I can still see Joe as he got into *Smoke Gets In Your Eyes.* He hit that switch, and pretty soon smoke was pouring out, those little things were exploding, he was coughing and gasping and belching . . . beautiful!

He didn't use that bit again for the run of the date.

Whitey Mitchell: In the old days of Charlie's Tavern, it was a smart idea to keep oneself in the good graces of Charlie Jacobs, the proprietor of that establishment. If he liked you, he would take your phone messages, cash your checks, put your dinners on the cuff, and even, if in his judgment you were a particularly promising musician, lend you money. But, if in his judgment, you were socially undesirable, he would not hesitate to prohibit you from crossing his threshold. A certain brilliant young trumpet player around town seemed to Charlie to be exhibiting tell-tale signs of deportment which, to put it mildly, has never received the approbation of the public at large, and so Charlie ushered him out of the Inn one day, with the admonition that he was never to return. The trumpeter was heard to mutter sadly, "What am I gonna do now? I've been banned from bars, and barred from bands."

Leonard Feather: A few years ago, in a burst of patriotism, I combined the talents of Red, Whitey and Blue Mitchell. Along with André Previn and a few others, they made an album under my supervision, with Gordon B. (Whitey) Mitchell as leader.

Whitey ordered several copies of the album to be sent to him by the company from time to time. The bills were invariably addressed to "Whitney Mitchell." The following is the text of an actual letter sent to the company soon afterward on the letterhead of Whitey's record company.

GEEBILL MUSIC PUBLISHERS
Hackensack, N.J.

MGM Records,   Dec. 1, 1958
1540 Broadway,
New York 36, N.Y.

Gentlemen:

I am inclosing the latest in a series of curious letters we have been receiving from you regarding our purchase of 15 copies of Metrojazz E 1012 LPs, which have all been addressed to one "Whitney Mitchell."

A thorough search of our Personnel Files fails to disclose that any such person is in our employ.

One of our officers helpfully suggests that perhaps you meant to address your inquiries to one "Whitey Mitchell" (just like the Whitey Mitchell whose LP it is, you fatheads), and that if this is the case, you may be assured that any letter so addressed will be received by the gentleman in question.

If I can be of any further assistance in this matter, please do not hesitate to call on me.

Sincerely,

Gordon B. Mitchell

PRESIDENT

(P.S. MGM Records got the name right from then on.)

Dick Hyman: There was a happy, party-like atmosphere at a daily radio show I played on in 1955–56. Allyn Edwards, followed by Bill Cullen, ran an early morning program on WNBC that used both recorded music and live music. The live orchestra was under the direction of Eddie Safranski.

We began at 7:05 a.m.; first the theme song, then we had time for a cup of coffee. The real point of the show, as far as we were concerned, was one that the listeners knew nothing about. The idea was to see how much socializing, coffee-drinking, jamming, rehearsing and unbroadcastable-joke-telling we could squeeze in, while the records and commercial transcriptions were being played, without missing a downbeat when the time came to do a live number.

The band included Will Bradley, Mick McMickle, Artie Baker, Hymie Schertzer, Al Kink, Mundell Lowe, Don Lamond, Safranski and myself. Eddie played bass and conducted.

One day we decided to up the stakes, without telling Safranski. We arranged with the engineer that on one of our numbers, instead of carrying our live performance, he would put on the air a SESAC transcription that the band had made of the same tune.

The number was announced, and we started to play it, live. Then about half-way through, we began goofing and playing all kinds of clinkers and generally tearing things to pieces, and finally the whole band staggered to a halt and we began shouting wild recriminations at each other.

Poor Safranski was turning six shades of green. His expression was indescribable. Meanwhile the record was spinning, of course, but Eddie didn't know this for what must have been an unbearable length of time.

Billy Taylor: When I first came to New York, nobody knew me. I was around 52nd Street, trying to be heard, and looking for a break. One day I was approached by a representative of Savoy Records. He gave me a big build-up, about how he'd heard all about me. That seemed odd, but I figured he must have been talking to a few musicians.

"We're going to give you a recording contract," he said, "and you'll be able to do anything you like."

"That sounds great!" I said, because I'd heard all about how so many recording companies try to change your style or your material.

"Sure," he said, "all you have to do is just be yourself."

Well, a couple of weeks later I went to the studio to make my very first record date, and I ran down the first tune and made a trial take.

The guy was still enthusiastic . . . but with reservations.

"That sounds fine!" he said. "But now would you try to play it a little more like Errol Garner?"

•

One of the most amazing bands I ever worked in was the so-called "Dream Band" that was specially assembled in the early 1950s for a week at Birdland. Everybody was in it—the personnel consisted almost entirely of sidemen who wanted to be leaders, or had been leaders from time to time. I think the trumpet section consisted of Dizzy Gillespie, Miles Davis, Fats Navarro, Kenny Dorham and Red Rodney; the trombones were J.J. Johnson, Kai Winding and Benny Green, and the saxes included Gerry Mullugan and Lee Konitz; the rhythm section was Art Blakey and Al McKibbon and myself.

They were all marvelous musicians and the solos were the greatest. The only trouble was that when they tried to play the arrangements (using Dizzy's big band book) they sounded awful.

Birdland wanted to bill it as "Dizzy Gillespie's Dream Band." But Dizzy said, "No, that's not my band, don't put it under my name." So they decided to use the name of Symphony Sid, who ran the radio show out of Birdland, and call it Symphony Sid's Dream Band. And Sid said, "No, don't put my name on it—I'm not responsible."

I guess none of the other musicians wanted their names on it either, so they just couldn't name a leader. They wound up calling it just "The Birdland Dream Band." That sure was a strange dream—I guess everybody was relieved when they woke up the following week.

:

Musicians find an odd range of pastimes with which to while away the hours between shows. One of the most contagious was derived a couple of years ago from an idea initiated by Freddy Schreiber, then the bassist with Cal Tjader's group.

Schreiber's hobby was the assembling of names for an imaginary all-star band. Many of the names in the following typical personnel were originally suggested by him:

TRUMPETS:	Chester Gigolo
	Felix Cited
	Darryl B. Morticome
	Lucius N. Savuma
TROMBONES:	Walter Walcarpitz
	Abner Selfabal
	Jim Nasium
SAXES:	Amos B. Haven
	Morey Ziduals
	Moe Zaic
	Baron Wasteland
	Sharon Sharalijk
PIANO:	Thelonious Galantown
BASS:	Voorhees A. Jollygoodfellow

DRUMS:	Arturo Verciz
GUITAR:	Manuel Lehba

The vocalist for this orchestra may be drawn from a large pool of available girl singers. Among them are Rachel Prejudice, Sonia Papermoon, Lois De Nominator, Barbara Seville, Sybil Rights, Freda Slaves and Marsha Dymes. Or they may all be assembled into a choral group, under the direction of Amanda B. Reckonwith.

André Previn: There was a rivalry going on between two trumpet players in the Stan Kenton band. They were at the Hollywood Palladium, and these two guys had been quarreling and jealous, and finally the thing came to a head, and one of them said, "All right, this is it," and took off his coat. And the other guy said, "Any time you say," and he handed his coat to another guy. So the two of them squared off for a fight. But just before the first punch was about to land, one of them stopped short and made the one remark only a trumpet player would make before a fight:

"Oh, by the way—not in the mouth, huh?"

And the other one said: "Oh, no!" And so, with their embouchures guaranteed, they went ahead and started the scrap.

:

Tony Martin was working in Las Vegas. There was a guy in the band there, I hear, who had the most phenomenal luck with the chicks in Vegas of anyone that ever lived. He was so amazing that the guys, for reasons which we won't go into, nicknamed him Clyde Beatty.

On the closing night of Tony's engagement, Tony was feeling pretty good, and onstage, as is customary for night club performers, he was thanking everybody in the world. You know—the producer and the lighting men and the band and so forth. Then, because he was kind of happy, he added: "And also, ladies and gentlemen, I want you to meet one of the great men of the world, Mr. Clyde Beatty."

And from the audience, the real Clyde Beatty got up and took a bow. How do you like that for odds?

143

When the guy got up and Tony realized it was really Clyde Beatty who'd stood up, he fell apart so completely he couldn't finish the show.

Charlie Barnet: At El Rancho in Las Vegas I had signed a contract for specific hours. The hours were bad enough, I think they were 11 until 4:30 in the morning, but when we get there Beldon Katelman says, "Your hours are from 12 until 6."

"Well, just a minute, Mr. Katelman," I said, "I presume that you're a businessman; you own all this place, and you run it, and I presume you read a contract before you sign it; I'm a goof, yet I do. The hours are as prescribed: we get through at 4:30."

We were at complete loggerheads. We went to work at 11:00. He had the doors closed, the lights off, the PA system turned off, and we played in there. We played *Dancing in the Dark.* We started out in C, and everybody took like two choruses, and then we went to D Flat and everybody took two choruses—we played *Dancing in the Dark* for a whole hour.

This went on, and finally he says "Tomorrow night, you play in the parking lot."

I sent a wire. I didn't know anybody in the Las Vegas union at the time, so I sent a direct wire to Petrillo and explained the situation—it was a very long wire—and he sent a wire back to Katelman and he says, "Special scale for bands playing in the parking lot; Sidemen, $1500 a week, Leader, $4500 a week." And that was when the lights went on again all over El Rancho. Yes, we finished our engagement—but I can't swear that we were held over.

Peggy Lee: We were rehearsing at my house one day with Stella Castellucci on harp and Gene Di Novi on piano and some others.

On one number there was some confusion because the other musicians had a lot of chord changes that didn't seem to be in Stella's part.

"There's something wrong here," said Stella. "I have a running F Major Seventh."

"Heavens!" said Gene, "and no doctor in the house!"

Charlie Barnet: Around 1938, right after our Famous Door engagement, we were playing the New Penn Club outside Pittsburgh. Andy Gibson was writing our arrangements. We were having a rehearsal there one afternoon. It was way out in the country, a sort of roadhouse; and a very bedraggled person came in, his shoes all spread out at the sides, and manuscripts under his arm and he wondered if we could run over an arrangement.

Well, this kind of thing was always happening to us, and in most cases the arrangements were pretty bad. But things had gone rather fast this afternoon, so I said, "Okay, let's have the arrangement, we'll pass it out."

There were groans and cries of "Oh, no!" from the band. But they started in. After the first four bars, they sat up straight in their chairs. After eight bars, the legs became uncrossed. By the end of the first chorus, everybody was blowing like they meant it. The arrangement was just great.

The unknown young gentleman, who at that time was playing trumpet and trombone in a horrible Lombardo type band called Baron Elliott in Bridgeport, was a fellow named Billy May. I hired him right on the spot.

It was one of the luckiest things I ever did, because he was the one that came up with *Cherokee* for me, and *Pompton Turnpike* and a lot of others that were very important to the band. The moral is: never judge an arranger by the condition of his shoes.

Later, in New York, one of the songpluggers tipped us off that Benny Goodman was looking for the guy that was writing our arrangements. And of course we couldn't begin to match the kind of money that Benny could pay him. So we formed a strategy.

We had Billy hidden away in a hotel room, and we gave him so much writing to do that he could hardly stop to think. We didn't even allow him out of the room; we had all the food sent in, and saw to it that Benny never got to him.

André Previn: When Mel Powell was working at MGM, he and I were very good friends. Once we had some time off. We hadn't seen snow in a long time; so Mel said, "I'll tell you what. I have some studying to do, and you have some work to do on some scores; now somebody has told me about a place up above Idyll-wild, very high up in the mountains, with a cabin. Let's go up there and tramp through the snow and relax."

So after Mel said to his wife, Martha Scott, "Why don't you pick us up in three days," we drove up there.

It was so deep in snow up there that I can't describe it; and the logs were all wet. I found a bottle of coal oil, and I said, "I think if we sprinkled this on the logs they would catch fire." And Mel said, "That's a marvelous idea; but they look pretty wet. Empty the whole bottle out in the fireplace."

We did, and lit a match.

Well, the whole thing just went up like the bridge on the River Kwai. We literally charred down one whole wall of the cabin—for which we had to pay—didn't burn ourselves, because we had thrown the match in; we were cowards. And we moved to another cabin.

Finally, by the third day, we were both so nervous from not having played the piano that we went to the man that owned the cabins and asked him whether he had a piano. And he said, "Well, there's an old upright piano over in the tool shed, which we bring out only for our summer guests. You can't play on it in there—it's dark and damp in there." So we said, well, suppose we move it over into the cabin? And he said that was just about impossible—it was something like five hundred yards, and the snow was up to our ears, practically, but still we said we'd try it.

So we got hold of this piano somehow between us and we got going. We eventually managed to drag it maybe a hundred or two hundred yards, and by that time both of us were utterly pooped. It was impossible; we were just about dead.

Mel said "Listen, it's a lovely night. Why don't we just play out here?"

I said "Fine." We had brought with us the Haydn Symphony for four hands, so I ran back to the cabin, got two flashlights, propped them up on the piano and we started playing.

It was so cold that we had to keep our gloves on, and we wore those wool hats that you pull down over the ears.

We were right in the middle of the third movement—I even remember which symphony it was, 104 in D Major—when Martha Scott drove up.

The tableau of the two of us, both sitting out there in the snow in a moonlit forest, at an old upright playing Haydn with our gloves on, was something she never got over, and especially the fact that we couldn't quite understand why she was so amazed. Because we were having a very good time.

I'm afraid the story has an anti-climax. We hired some people to schlepp the piano back.

Gerald Wilson: You remember the old showmanship bits we used to do in the Lunceford band? There was that one part in Sy Oliver's *For Dancers Only* when the brass would play a series of triplets, then we'd all throw our horns up in the air and twirl them before we resumed playing.

One night we were playing Loew's State Theater in New York and my enthusiasm, I guess, got the better of me. We reached that part, I threw my trumpet up for the big twirl, and pow! right out into the audience, sailing over the heads of several scared customers and finally landing without injuring anyone, or anything, except itself.

I've been a little scared of triplets ever since.

Sascha Burland: I recall a big band date I was producing for a jingle. We had a magnificent line-up of jazz stars. Throughout the date the guys were talking shop about instruments: remarks like "Mine has a fast-playing neck" and "I prefer a big bore" were bandied about the studio.

The time came for a take, and since we were trying for a real snapping sound on the second and fourth beats, the singers started snapping their fingers. After about 30 takes of a very complicated arrangement, blisters were being raised.

It was then that Nick Travis, the trumpeter, leaned over to one of the singers and remarked, "Say, that's a pretty good snap. What kind of finger do you use?"

Georgie Auld: Bunny Berigan used to have a favorite expression when it was time to crack another bottle. "Bring on the dancing team," he'd say to the bandboy. The team was Haig and Haig.

Jack Tracy: It happened at a jam session in Philadelphia in 1945. Some of the modern local guys were playing a private Sunday afternoon affair, and things were swinging.

Louis Jordan was playing in town, and someone had invited him to fall by. He walked in, horn in hand, played a frantic 10-minute solo that had the place in an uproar, walked offstand with a puzzled look, and said, "Man, what was that tune we were playing?"

:

A Hollywood agent named Red Doff called me one day to extoll the talents of an artist he represented and to inquire if I would be interested in the man recording-wise. "What does he do?" I wondered.

"Among other things," said Red, "he can sing and play in ten different languages."

:

One year Mercury Records taped the Indianapolis "500" classic to issue in their "sounds" series. Driver Tony Bettenhausen was one of the experts they had to help assemble the final master. As he was working on the tapes at the recording studio, some musicians heard the strange sounds and dropped in to listen.

"Listen to those engines," Tony exulted as cars roared by. "Listen, you can hear my car coming down the stretch," he said, as a car screamed by in stereo. "What did you think of that?"

Bassist Johnny Frigo replied, "Sounded as if you were rushing the tempo a little."

Roy Eldridge: One time when I was playing with Artie Shaw's band, we were having some problems on a record date. If I'm not mistaken, the tune was *Someone To Watch Over Me,* and we had made so many bad starts and unusable takes, number 38 was coming up.

One of the saxophone players looked up at Artie and said very reasonably, "Maybe if we went on to something else—leave this alone for a while—it would work out better."

Shaw looked at the whole band and said, "Anybody who doesn't like the way I'm running this band can pick up his horn and leave."

I took the mouthpiece out of my horn and stood up, and Shaw yelled, "I didn't mean you!"

George Frazier: Charles Ellsworth (Pee Wee) Russell is a spindly-shaped man with a long, seamed face, the perpetual shakes, and a genius that time has not noticeably withered. Years ago, a *Time* magazine writer with a pseudo-Groton accent interviewed Eddie Condon and, in the course of his questioning, asked, "Now what about Pee Wee? (He pronounced it 'Payway.') Is he draftable?"

Condon raised a shocked eyebrow. "Payway?" he said. "If the Japs should happen to invade the ice-skating rink at Rockefeller Plaza, Payway is a cinch to be called up for limited service."

Mezz Mezzrow: Pee Wee Russell and Bix Beiderbecke shared a cottage in Hudson Lake, Indiana, one summer while they were playing with Jean Goldkette.

One day, it seems, Bix and Pee Wee decided they needed some rubber, so they bought this old Buick for thirty-five bucks. It wasn't running then—so far as any of us knew, it never *did* run—but those two Barney Oldfields weren't stumped. They pushed it all the way our to their cottage and there it squatted forever after; nobody even tried to budge it again. It made a good, sturdy shaving rack, though, and the boys were happy with it. They figured that to live right in the country you had to have a car.

Dom Cerulli: Trumpeter Bobby Hackett still blushes when he talks about the solo part he recorded with Jackie Gleason's big orchestra for one of the comedian's mood-music albums. "We had done take after take," says Hackett, "and something always happened to ruin it every time. Finally, we were coming into the last figure of what sounded like a perfect take. I put my horn to my

149

Pee Wee Russell

lips, got in close to the mike for a final cadenza, and my wrist-watch alarm went off, right into the microphone! The band broke up, but Gleason looked as if he was going to cry."

:

At the 1963 awards banquet in New York held by NARAS (the National Academy of Recording Arts and Sciences), well-wishers were congratulating Stan Getz for winning a "Grammy" for his hit record of *Desafinado*. One of them poked Stan in the ribs and commented, "You've got big as a house, Stan. How much weight did you put on?"

Getz replied, "Oh . . . about thirty thousand dollars."

:

Writer James T. Maher attended a luncheon at which he was taken in hand by Professor Marshall Stearns, head of the Institute of Jazz Studies, who introduced him to Duke Ellington. Ellington gallantly acknowledged the introduction.

"You know, Duke," Professor Stearns said, "I've been introducing you to Jim a once a year for at least the last five years."

Without losing a beat, Duke smiled and said: "And it's been a greater pleasure every time."

Bob Bach: Did you ever hear about the time they held the Olympic Games on 52nd Street? This story involves the fabulous Neem. His real name was Henry Nemo; he wrote the 1938 Cotton Club show with Duke Ellington, as well as *Don't Take Your Love From Me* and a lot of other good songs. But he was best known around Broadway as one of the first experts in double talk and one of the wildest characters ever.

One time Nemo briefly became a bandleader and fronted a group at one of the small spots along 52nd Street. Business was terrible; very few people cared about hearing the Great Neem.

One night, when the place was particularly uninhabited, he stopped the music cold in the middle of a chorus. "Now," he said, "we will present our own version of the Olympic Games. First: the discus throw."

With that, he picked up some plates off the tables and began hurling them over the bandstand.

151

"Next," he said, "the broad jump," and he lined up some chairs and leaped over them.

"And now," he concluded, "the hundred yard dash." He knelt down for a sprinter's start, got a big roll going on the drums, dashed right through the tables and out the front door, and disappeared into a club across the street. And that was the last anyone saw of the Neem as a performer on 52nd Street.

Shorty Sherock: Horace Heidt was one of the bandleaders who really made it financially. He had a beautiful big place out in the Valley, and he had his own chickens there, and a house designed by Frank Lloyd Wright, I think, and he invited the band out for a Christmas party. It was too cold to swim in his fine pool and we didn't visit his private bomb shelter, but drinks were passed around in these great big zombie glasses and Heidt made a touching little speech.

"I want to thank you all," he said, "for your hard work in the band and all the fine cooperation we've had from you during the year. I'd like to present each of you with a token of my appreciation."

And as we filed out, wondering whether it would be gold watches or what, he handed each of us—a dozen freshly laid eggs.

A few weeks later there was an item in *Down Beat* that read something like this: "Members of Horace Heidt band who received eggs, and members of Harry James band who received a fifth of Scotch, would like to meet band that received milk for Christmas. Object: egg nog."

Antics With Semantics: Probably the first of the hip jazz stories was the one about the musician who sat down at a lunch counter and asked for an order of cherry pie.

"The cherry pie is gone," said the counterman.

"Crazy! I'll take two pieces!"

        :

A similar lack of rapport was noted by *Down Beat* in connection with an attempt by Paul Desmond to buy a dacron blanket.

"I'm sorry, sir," said the salesgirl, "We seem to be all out of dacron blankets. But wouldn't you like to look at this one?

"No. I don't think so. I want a dacron."

"But, sir, this one is down. It's real down."

"I'm hip," said Desmond. "But I still want a dacron."

:

Jimmy Dorsey once had a band boy, Eddie, who was noted for his Charlie's Tavern approach to the English language. One of his most celebrated gaffes, said to have been committed on several occasions, ran roughly as follows:

Eddie: This wine ain't so great if you ask me.

Dorsey: What are you, a connoisseur or something?

Eddie: No, I'm not sore—I just don't dig the wine.

Perhaps the most striking example of the succinct use of jazz terminology can be found in a story involving Dodo Marmarosa, the talented young bop star of the 1940s, who was brilliantly expressive at the piano though less than completely articulate in other areas.

Dodo was playing at Billy Berg's club in Hollywood. Between sets he was trying to strike up an acquaintance with a young lady. She apparently wanted no part of him, and when Dodo returned to the bandstand she mentioned the incident to her escort, who had just returned to the table.

The escort waited for Dodo to come outside after the next set, then proceeded to beat him mercilessly. When the musicians were unable to find Dodo as the time for the following set drew near, somebody rushed into the club to report that he had been found outside.

The musicians found Dodo lying helpless in the parking lot, bleeding profusely. As they leaned over him and tried to administer first aid and solace, one of them asked him what had happened.

Dodo's only answer was: "Man, what a drag!"

:

Steve Allen was interviewing some of the members of his TV audience one evening, and came to a little girl about five years old.

"Do you go to school?"

"No, not yet."

"What do you do with yourself all day?"

"Well, I go out in the garden."

"And what do you do in the garden?"

"I dig," said the little girl.

"I'm hip," said Steve.

:

During the 1950s there was a fad for anecdotes about a pair of purely fictional characters known as "the two beboppers." Many of these were reported in Robert Sylvester's column in the *New York Daily News*.

One of the best known tells of the night the two beboppers were standing on a 25th floor rooftop, high in more senses than one. Suddenly one of them ran to the edge and jumped off. The police soon picked up the other, who didn't seem at all perturbed by the fatal accident to his buddy.

"How could you let him do a thing like that?" he was asked.

"Well, pops," the bopper decided after giving the matter some thought, "I really believed he could make it."

:

It was also reported that two beboppers were walking along a country road when there was a huge crash. An enormous bell had fallen from the belfry of a church and landed on the sidewalk.

One bopper turned around, startled. "What was that?"

The other, without looking back, replied: "F Sharp."

:

Two boppers met on the street and one introduced the other to his wife, who was about as attractive as Bela Lugosi. At a subsequent meeting the bopper asked his pal how he could have married such a homely woman.

The husband was aghast. "Man!" he demanded, "don't you dig distortion?"

:

Two beboppers, standing at an intersection in Brooklyn, saw a car crash into a tree, throwing the driver clear. Sliding toward the boppers, the driver skimmed 25 feet on his stomach and ended, unconscious, at the curb. Said one bopper:

"Safe!"

:

One day the two boppers found themselves walking through a country cemetery. The sun was sinking low in the west, the grass on the graves was neatly clipped, lovely flowers marked the headstones, and soft music could be heard from the nearby church.

"Man," said the first bopper, "these cats really know how to live."

:

The two boppers were standing outside Junior's, the celebrated bar and musicians' rendezvous. The first bopper entered and invited the other to join him.

"I can't, man," he explained. "I'm on vacation."

:

One bop musician had a small daughter who was reported one day to have been overheard picking petals from a daisy to the following refrain:

"He digs me, got no eyes, digs me, got no eyes, digs me, got no eyes . . ."

:

The boppers went to the Central Park Zoo and saw a lion, tossing its head with a mighty roar. "Come on, man," said one. "I've seen enough. Let's split." "What?" demanded the other, "and miss the picture?"

Robert Sylvester: Joe Rushton is a well known musician from Chicago whose main instrument has always been the bass saxophone. Joe was in love with a motorcycle. He would strap his big horn on his back and ride the motor bike to all dates. When he joined the Benny Goodman band in 1942, however, he had to ride the Goodman band bus, so he was obliged to leave the motorcycle on blocks in a garage.

When he came back from a long road tour, Eddie Condon asked him if he had been riding his motorcycle lately. "No," said Rushton sadly, "but I did have a chance to go back and sit on it for a while."

Some time soon after, a group of musicians went to a party and

Joe brought his bike and his horn. The host had a tape recorder and Joe wanted to cut some sides. But Condon and the other musicians were concentrating on other matters and didn't feel like starting a session. So Joe finally took the tape machine out on the porch—and got a beautiful hi-fi recording of his motorcycle.

:

Eddie Condon once called me to say that he had a 65-year-old aunt coming to town. This nice old lady had never seen a musical and Eddie wanted to get her a pair of tickets for *Wonderful Town* on Saturday night. I said I couldn't help. Condon said it was essential; the lady was 65 years old and he wanted her to see this show.

"If it's that important," I told him, "we can go to the speculators and pay $50 a seat."

Condon thought this over.

"No," he decided at last. "After all, she's only 65."

Louis Armstrong: The Zulus Club was the first colored carnival club to get together in New Orleans. The Club has for generations consisted of the fellows in my neighborhood . . . The members were coal cart drivers, bar tenders, waiters, hustlers etc., people of all walks of life . . . Nobody had very much . . . But they loved each other.

It was my lifelong ambition to become King of the Zulus in the Mardi Gras parade some day . . . and the Lord certainly did answer my prayer.

The day before I stepped up on that float, which was Mardi Gras day, I payed the Mayor a visit, and had quite a few pictures made with him in his office. I met the Mayor through a friend of mine . . . Negro by the name of Bo Zo . . .

After we had a long chat before the microphone, before an office full of people, the Mayor said—Satchmo—I read in the Time Magazine where you said—all you wanted to do was to be the King of the Zulus, and you were ready to die . . . is that true? . . .

I said—yes Mr. Mayor,—but there ain't no use of the Lord taking me *literally*!

•

Most jazz fans never have been able to understand why Louis Armstrong for years has maintained that one of his favorite bands is Guy Lombardo. Louis once explained his choice this way: "This cat in New York asked me to pick my favorite bands, so I had Guy Lombardo in there. He said, 'Are you sure?' so I told him that old one we always used to say, 'I never let my mouth say nothin' that my head can't stand'."

•

In 1953 Charlie Parker worked a series of concerts promoted in collaboration with Robert George Reisner at the Open Door in Greenwich Village.

One evening between sets Reisner heard a most unpleasant sound coming from the bandstand. He turned around and saw a group performing, in a manner not far removed from that of the typical rock 'n' rollers, a number that was as far from the Open Door's musical policy as Elvis Presley from Billie Holiday.

Reisner told the leader he was not suited to this audience and asked that the combo leave the stand.

"But," he was told, "Charlie Parker hired us."

Incredulous, Reisner checked the facts with Bird. Sure enough, it turned out to be true. "But why would you hire a bunch like that? The people don't dig them; I'll have to get rid of them."

"Bob," Parker answered, "you just don't understand business methods. Those cats are so bad that instead of having a full house we'll soon have the room half-empty and leave more room for the people that are waiting to get in. This will give us the turnover."

"Bird," said Reisner, "you're a better business man than I realized."

:

Shortly before the final attack that killed him, a doctor was examining Charlie Parker. Bird had a tremendous capacity for liquor of almost any sort, and was not a bit hesitant about testing it.

When the doctor asked him if he drank much, Bird's reply was a classic understatement:

"I enjoy an occasional sherry before dinner," he said.

157

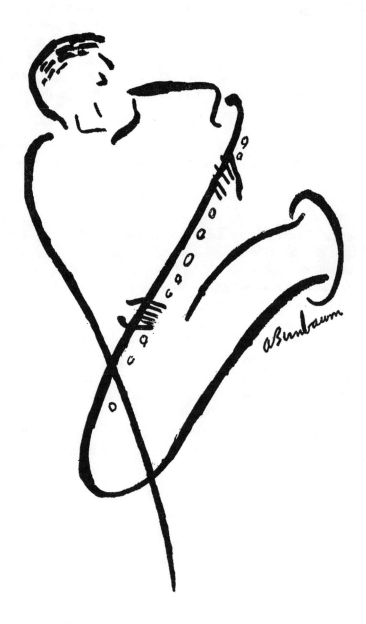

Gerry Mulligan

:

A constant problem at record dates is to find new titles for original instrumental tunes composed for, or improvised during, the session.

Gerry Mulligan is one musician who seems unlikely ever to run out of good title ideas. It was he who, in dedicating a number to the disc jockey fraternity, named it *Nights At The Turntable.* Teamed with Johnny ("Rabbit") Hodges for a two-saxophone album, he came up with an opus called *Eighteen Carrots For Rabbit.*

Mulligan records are responsible for two of the outstanding spoonerism titles. Using the chord sequence of *Strike Up The Band,* Jeru and his combo cut an original titled *Bike Up The Strand.* On a more recent album session his girl friend, Judy Holliday, was responsible for the best title suggestion of the day: *Blight Of The Fumble Bee.*

On one Mulligan big band date, Al Cohn brought in an instrumental that was released under the title *Lady Chatterley's Mother.* The LP cut by Jeru with Paul Desmond, whose sense of humor runs along the same line as Mulligan's, produced such numbers as *Battle Hymn Of The Republican.*

Even when not obviously funny, Mulligan's titles often have a latent humor, as was obliquely pointed out in Nat Hentoff's liner notes to the Mulligan-Desmond LP. *Standstill,* described as containing an "intimation of a figurative coronary occlusion," was based on the chords of *My Heart Stood Still. Fall Out* was called "a hortatory celebration of natural genetics rather than an essay on possible genocide." It was based on the chords of *Let's Fall In Love.*

:

From a British newspaper story about how Mulligan addressed a London audience during concert at Royal Festival Hall:

"Gerry started talking to the audience to bring them in closer. He was just kidding around in that cracker-barrel kind of humor he reserves for the public when quite suddenly, during a quiet moment, he said, apropos of nothing at all, 'And about our foreign policy; you can't blame that on me.' "

:

Overheard at Shelly's Manne Hole—a conversation between two flute fans:

Sam Most enthusiast (intensely): Most is the man!

Herbie Mann follower (angrily): Mann is the most!

:

Among the best sources of stories in the jazz world are pianist Erroll Garner and his aggressive, loyally single-minded manager, Martha Glaser.

Martha relates everything solely to the music world—this was demonstrated at a party once in Providence, R.I., when she was introduced to a young man named Keith Stewart. "Keith," she was told, "has the best record of any jockey at Narragansett this year."

"That's wonderful," said Martha, and turning to Stewart, "what station did you say you were with?"

:

Once a night club owner, not too well informed but anxious to impress, told Martha proudly of the piano he had found for Erroll's next engagement." We'll have a 5′8″ piano for him this time," he declared, beaming.

With a straight face, Martha said: "I'm sorry, but Erroll's only 5′2″."

Crestfallen, the manager said: "Gee, maybe we can exchange it."

:

Before one of his overseas tours, Erroll was recalcitrant when Martha insisted that a vaccination was necessary. "If you don't get one you could contract smallpox," she warned him. To which Erroll's reply was a plaintive: "So how come you want to send me to places where I can get sick?"

:

Eddie Condon, in his *Treasury of Jazz,* related a Tommy Dorsey story that he heard from Jimmy Dorsey.

It seems that Tommy Dorsey, Jr. was a substitute on the Williams football team, and Tommy went down to Princeton to see him play. Sitting next to Tommy was an old Williams graduate, complete with flask and spirit. Tommy was glum throughout most of the game, for Tommy Jr. was kept on the bench. Finally he was sent in, and his name was announced on the loudspeaker, Tommy sat up, full of fatherly pride. The old Williams man peered at him closely.

"That your boy, there?" he inquired.

"Yes, sir," said Tommy, "that's my boy."

"You the bandleader?" the o.g. asked.

"Yeah," said Tommy, trying to keep his mind on the game.

"What fraternity's he in at Williams?"

"I don't know," said Tommy.

"What do you mean, you don't know?"

Tommy's well-known Irish was rising. "I don't know," he said. "I knew once, but I forgot."

"Why don't you know?" the Williams pest persisted.

"Listen," said Tommy, "why the hell should I know?"

"Why," said the old grad, "I've got all *your* records."

:

During the swing band years there was one well-known leader (let's call him Sid Hassel) whose reluctance to part with a dollar was legendary. No less characteristic of him was a chronic inability to keep track of his itinerary while the band was on tour.

Gradually he evolved a system that enabled him to save money, keep finding out where his next bookings were, and even check on the salary his agent had arranged for him, all without spending a penny.

He would make a long distance, person-to-person call to the office of his booking agent in New York, but instead of asking for the agent he would ask for Sid Hassel.

The answer would come: "I'm sorry, but Mr. Hassel is not here."

"Do you know where I can reach him?"

"I believe he'll be at the Roosevelt Hotel in New Orleans from August 5 through August 10."

Next, to check on his salary, Hassel would ask: "Can you tell me what room he will be in at the hotel?"

"He will be staying in Room 2250."

One day this system almost broke down. Told that the room number would be 1750, Hassel said, "Can't you make that 2000?"

:

Buddy Bregman was conducting an orchestra comprising the best of the Hollywood musicians. The arrangement contained one bar in ⁵⁄₄ time, but Buddy didn't quite know how to conduct a ⁵⁄₄ bar. The proceedings kept falling apart. Buddy even gave instructions to the orchestra: "Those of you who have anything on the first beat, just wait for me;" and his hands would remain motionless for the first beat, after which he resumed conducting in ⁴⁄₄.

During a five minute break André Previn, who happened to be visiting the studio, took him to one side and offered to show him how to conduct a ⁵⁄₄ bar.

Bregman was totally unperturbed. "Thanks very much," he said, "but there's no need to bother. The hell with it; I'll just never write another ⁵⁄₄ bar."

:

For some years Bill and Lloyd Ulyate have led a band at Disneyland. To simplify the pronunciation and spelling, they bill the band as "Elliott Brothers Orchestra."

The ambiguity in this never became apparent until one day when a small fan approached Lloyd with the meek request:

"May I have your autograph, please, Mr. Brothers?"

And Shelly Manne swears that during an evening at the Manne Hole, his Hollywood club, an enthusiastic youngster shook hands with him and said warmly:

"Thank you for a most enjoyable evening, Mr. Manhole."

14

I invented Bossa Nova!

by Prof. S. Rosentwig McSiegel

And now I'd like to play the number that's going to send my kids through college—*Dis Here Finado.*

Stan Getz

• • • • • • • •

The Irish philosopher and wit Patrick O'Latunji once observed that "facts are stubborn things." No facts have been more recalcitrant, or slower in emerging, than the truth about what is now known as Bossa Nova.

For the past couple of years I have sat back quietly, maintaining a dignified calm while the jackals have devoured and demolished an art form for which I have never attempted to take any credit. But a man can take only just so much. The time has come to speak out with, if I may borrow an old New England expression, vigor.

The fact that I was single-mouthedly responsible for bossa nova will, of course, be glibly ignored by the mythstorians. This kind of thing, of course, is no new experience for me. When soul music emerged I let Horace Silver take all the credit. Though my own funk was known for miles around and had established me as the No. 1 Pole Cat, I recalled wistfully the words of Elizabeth Barrett Browning: "I should not dare to call my soul my own." According to Bartlett's, she wrote this in a book called *Ibid,* and I can understand just how she felt.

The truth about Bossa Nova goes back to the early days of the riverboats. After I had given up hope of ever teaching Bunk Johnson the right changes to *Free as a Bird* (a tune later popularized in slightly altered form by Sleepy Matsumoto), I abandoned my New Orleans teaching gigs and fled, as a bird, to New England.

Although Boston at that time had segregated unions, I was able with the help of careful makeup and a slight change of name (to McSweeney) to arrange transfer to the Gentile Local 793625. (At first there was considerable resentment among officials of Local 710814, Boston B'nai B'rith, who felt this was an example of reverse discrimination, or Crow Jew.)

The Massachusetts Bay Line was then employing combos regularly on its nightly runs northward to New Hampshire, and I lost no time in determining that sousaphone players within 793625's jurisdiction were in very short supply. It was not long, either, before I discovered that they were in even shorter demand.

In any case, for three months I had to sweat out my card. Unable to ply my true trade, I killed time manufacturing surgical equipment for George Wein's father, scouting second-hand clothes for George Frazier, and baby-sitting for the parents of Harry Carney (who at that time was letting the baritone saxophone hold *him*). Boston, like New Orleans, had its Storyville, but economic conditions in the sporting houses were so poor that the area in which they were located was known as the Red Ink District. (Storyville ultimately was closed down by order of George Wein, the surgeon's son.) In those days, however, there were still a few jobs available, and as soon as my three months were up I joined Pete Moss and his five-piece trio (cornet, banjo, tuba, player piano and Sideman) at one of the District's most exclusive fun palaces. A branch office of Pete Lala's, the fabled New Orleans house of kicks, it was operated by a cousin of Mahogany Hall's famous Lulu White. At first they called it Mahogany Hall East; later, to add a personal touch, they changed it to Lulu Lala's.

Word about our exotic rhythms spread like a smudge fire. One of our biggest request numbers was a riff tune I had dreamed up entitled *Shave and a Haircut Two Cents* (this wasn't in pre-inflation days: this was *before* pre-inflation.) One night a dramatic and entirely fortuitous change was brought about in our rending of this tune. As I was about to go into the final note of the basic figure, a slight earth tremor shook the neighborhood. As a result, I played it slightly behind the beat, so that what had been

came out

It was not long before this evolved into

Before long our novel approach to this opus, by then the virtual national anthem of the short hair jazz school, created a great demand for the trio. A critic in the *Christian Science Monitor* described us as "lambently angular." *Metronome,* then a brass band publication, hailed us as "coruscatingly opaque." Nat Hentoff, then a mere infant hanging around the bandstand, had fewer words at his command and had to settle for "ecstatically inchoate." On the strength of these encomiastic panegyrics, it was not long before a scout from the Massachusetts Bay Line spotted us and we were set for a trial run aboard the S.S. *Dill Picou.*

At that time the riverboats were plying regularly between Boston, Portsmouth and Dover, N.H. As we developed our style, we noticed in listeners' reactions a curious relationship to its temblor-induced origin: there was a sharp upsurge in the seasickness rate. But those who were able to remain vertical around the bandstand invariably asked the identical fascinated question: "What kind of lambently angular music is that you're playing?"

Since we had no name for it, it occurred to me that the two terminal points on our nightly route would make as good a handle as any. "This," I answered one evening in response to the usual question, "is Boston-Dover."

The rest, of course, is history. By the classic process of elision the t and d were eliminated and Bossa Nova was born.

But this was just the beginning. After the popularity of riverboat music had run, if I may coin a phrase, out of steam, we all drifted westward and found ourselves in Culver City, California, playing background music on movie lots, where tear-inducing moods were required by the stars of the old silents. One of these stars was John Gilbert, then playing opposite Greta Garbo. His peculiarly high-pitched nasal voice seemed unsuited to talking pictures, which were then ready to emerge, but ideal for the Boston-Dover style, with a dashing Latin touch added. Persuading him to change his name to Joao Gilberto, I accompanied him on his first trip to Rio. But language problems came between us. Every time he said "Obrigado" I assumed he wanted backing and began playing an ad lib obbligato. Need I tell you? I was fired and sent home in ignominy. The rest, of course, is hysteria.

My part was soon forgotten. The road of the pioneer is ever hard. Who today, for example, remembers my 1912 prediction that jazz could not continue to be confined to ¾ and ⁵⁄₄ time, that an effort would have to be made to transmute the idiom into a ⁴⁄₄ feeling? For all you can read about it in the history books it might never have happened. And who wrote the note that Cole Porter used for the verse of *Night and Day*, the note that then inspired Antonio Carlos Jobim to create his original *One Note Samba*? Most significant of all, which group was it that spent its entire career playing *Slightly Out of Tune*?

But that's life. The poor grow weak, and the rich grow strong, and them that has, Getz. But I still maintain I was the first musician with the new flair, regardless of race, Creed or Taylor.

Any time you want the whole truth, don't take my word for it. Just check the facts with George Wein's father.

15

Special announcement

Ladies and gentlemen, Birdland is honored to have in the house this evening none other than Mr. Marlo Brandon.

Pee-Wee Marquette

• • • • • • • •

One of the problems that constantly besets musicians is that of dealing with squares who, never having heard of them, manage to garble their names in posters, signs outside clubs, or announcements on the air. Musicians themselves, of course, are no less gifted in the art of saying the wrong thing at the right time.

One of the best known examples of this lack of perception victimized Kai Winding when he was playing trombone in the Stan Kenton orchestra around 1946. The band was on the air one night during a midwestern tour when the announcer blithely introduced an item on the program as follows:

"This next number will feature lovely Kai Winding. . . ."

When Jimmy Dorsey's orchestra was on the air regularly with Bing Crosby, a fair amount of dialogue was assigned to Jimmy, even though his ability at reading scripts was none too good.

One evening a celebrated, rather dignified, (and somewhat overweight) female opera star was featured on the program. Jimmy managed to get through his banter with Crosby, but when the time came to introduce the guest it came out like this:

"And now we bring you that great opera steer . . ."

That, incidentally, was the last program on which Jimmy was given lines.

Shorty Sherock recalls a broadcast from Kansas City by a territory band in which he was playing in the 1930s. The leader had taken the precaution, in order to be at ease on the air, of swallowing a nembutal pill. He also made the mistake of washing it down with a healthy slug of Scotch.

"Good evening, ladies and gentlemen," he said as the band played its opening theme. "We're going to start out by playing the goddamndest tune you ever heard in your life."

The band went off the air 29 minutes too early to play its closing theme.

Louis Armstrong, an incorrigible ad libber, was a guest on the

Dorsey Brothers' television series in the late 1950s when he introduced a number with an admonition that has become a classic in music circles.

"Don't forget the tempo, fellas," he said. "Not too slow, not too fast; just half-fast."

If there were a hall of fame for perpetrators of special announcements, there can be no doubt that the place of honor would be reserved for the unvanquished champion, who stands a firm 3 ft. 6 in. and weighs in at 100 lb. This is William Clayton "Pee-Wee" Marquette, master of ceremonies at Birdland almost continuously since the club was founded in 1949. Marquette during the 1950s was as indispensable a part of the Birdland mystique as the drawings of jazzmen on the wall, the sound of Shearing's *Lullaby* on the bandstand or the sight of the manager, Oscar Goodstein, at the foot of the stairs.

As an emcee Marquette has delighted and amused the famous, who find him cute and quaint, but has disturbed and confused the formalists, who feel that his contribution changes the tone of the room through his resemblance to a barker at a sideshow. Whatever one's reaction to Pee-Wee, it would be hard to control one's admiration for his uncommon mastery of the English language, which would do Mrs. Malaprop proud.

Not long after a plaque had been presented to Terry Gibbs for his victory in the vibraharp category of a magazine poll, Pee-Wee introduced him with a typical verbal flourish: "And now we would like to introduce a gentleman who has just been awarded the plague by *Down Beat*."

On another occasion, in his inimitable stentorian altissimo fortissimo, he announced: "We got a real famous celebrity with us in the house tonight, folks. It's none other than Oscar (dramatic pause) . . . no, not Goodstein, *Hammer*stein!"

Pee-Wee is never at a loss for little surprises with which to shake his audiences out of their complacency. Bassist Teddy Kotick, of Charlie Parker's combo, was once introduced to Birdlanders as "Teddy Kotex." During one of Dinah Washington's engagements Pee-Wee proudly drew himself up to his full height and said: "Next, Birdland is happy to present the one and only

Miss Ruth Brown!" It is reported that he has been incurably apprehensive of Miss Washington ever since.

Pee-Wee, born in 1919 in Montgomery, Alabama, has a long show business background. At 16 he was offered a job singing and dancing with a white band in Tennessee; to make this legally feasible, because he was a minor and a Negro, a special act had to be passed through the State legislature. He also worked for a while with Earl Hines' band. But Pee-Wee has a deep love of Broadway and of people; his happiest associations have been the night club emceeing days, first at the Zanzibar and the Royal Roost, then at Birdland, where his incumbency was immortalized by Blue Note's recordings at the club (". . . when you buy the record, folks, you'll hear your hands, so remember to applaud!")

Marquette's feelings are subject to easy bruises and he is quick to show them. After announcing "Count Basie and his 16-piece stereophonic band," he got into some mysterious verbal tangle one night with a Basie trombonist. The sentence he imposed on this malefactor was severe: he read him out of the band, speaking in his next announcement of "Count Basie and his _15_-piece stereophonic band."

Early Birdland employees claim that Pee-Wee's finest hour and greatest challenge occurred on the night when he was asked to read a table card designed to keep audiences quiet during performances by the soft-voiced Jeri Southern. The announcement read: "Proclamation! Cognoscenti of the Birdland Arts are hereby importuned to forego requisitioning of _vins et viands_ during the recital of Miss Jeri Southern, to effectuate the maximum benefits from her volatile variations in vocalization. There will be a hiatus in service, seating and side-issues during her renditions, with full restoration of such facilities following the denouement of her inimitable delineations." The message was signed: "William Clayton Marquette, Curator."

Pee-Wee's ghost writer had a short career. After one bout with this verbal cabbage before the first set, the curator decided to skip it. Had it been recorded, a tape of his one encounter with the polysyllables could have become Birdland's all-time bestseller.

Stan Kenton best summed up Pee-Wee Marquette's contribution to jazz history when he observed: "Until you've been introduced by Pee-Wee Marquette, you've just never been introduced at all."

André Previn: Ella Fitzgerald and I are very good friends; I'm sure she must know by now how I feel about her, so she won't mind my telling this story.

I did a record date for her when she was still with Decca. It was the first time she had ever sung with strings, and it knocked her out. From that time on she was always very fond of me, and I've often played for her and written for her. She used to have trouble with my name; it was some kind of a block; she just couldn't get it right.

A few years ago she was at the Fairmont in San Francisco; I had just given a concert with the San Francisco Symphony, and afterwards Dory and I, and Herb Caen, went to the Fairmont to see Ella. I was still in full dress, white tie and all.

Ella came out, and in the middle of her show she saw us, sitting ringside. And after the next number she said: "Ladies and gentleman, I want to take a moment to introduce someone to you." And she went into an absolute eulogy. She said: "This man is such a great musician and he makes me nervous by just sitting there and I adore him and I want you all to join me in giving a very hearty welcome to that great star, Andy Purvis." There was absolutely dead silence, broken only by the laughter of the three of us; a couple of people kind of half-heartedly clapped, probably thinking to themselves who the hell is Andy Purvis. I never had the heart to tell her this.

In the audience that night, unbeknownst to Ella, was Danny Kaye. I've worked with Danny often; and from that day, a good five or six years ago, he's never called me anything but Andy Purvis.

Bill Russo: *(The following is an actual announcement that Bill Russo used to make to concert audiences before one of his compositions was to be played by the Stan Kenton orchestra, in which Russo worked as composer-arranger and trombonist.)*

This composition is entitled *Ennui,* and it was originally meant to express a rather quiet and relaxed mood. There are some brass punctuations in the middle, and the whole thing becomes rather climactic after awhile. The main theme is stated by the trombone and is interrupted only by the short orchestral portions in the middle.

I think I might take a second to delve into the cosmological and metaphysical aspects of this composition. I think we can say quite simply that the transcendental character of the composition is based on two very definitely Freudian concepts, the first of which has to do with what we might call the continuant. The whole relationship between the first portion of this composition and the French horns as used in the second portion finds its roots in the philosophy of certain early Greek composers. The dichotomy between the Russians and the Ukrainians is a clear example of the lugubrious tendency of early Greek art. The whole relationship between this concept and certain basic concepts, say, of James Joyce is the fact that motorcycle riders find salted pop corn extremely good under those conditions.

Epilogue

Thank you, ladies and gentleman, for those kind applause.

Lionel Hampton